THE HISTORICAL SERIES OF THE REFORMED CHURCH IN AMERICA,
IN COOPERATION WITH
ORIGINS STUDIES IN DUTCH-AMERICAN HISTORY

NO. 52

SON OF SECCESSION
DOUWE J. VANDER WERP

Janet Sjaarda Sheers

WILLIAM B. EERDMANS PUBLISHING COMPANY
Grand Rapids, MI / Cambridge, U. K.

Wm. B. Eerdmans Publishing Co.
255 Jefferson Ave. S. E., Grand Rapids, Michigan 49503/
P.O. Box 163, Cambridge, CB3 9PU U.K.
www.eerdmans.com

Printed in the United States of America

Cover photos:

upper left, Graafschap Christian Reformed Church
lower right, Douwe J. Vander Werp
background, Reformed Church in Deersum, the Netherlands

To Gerrit W. Sheeres,

my husband and dearest friend

The Historical Series of the Reformed Church in America

The series was inaugurated in 1968 by the General Synod of the Reformed Church in America acting through the Commission on History to communicate the church's heritage and collective memory and to reflect on our identity and mission, encouraging historical scholarship which informs both church and academy.

General Editor,
> The Rev. Donald J. Bruggink, Ph.D, D.D.
> Western Theological Seminary
> Van Raalte Institute, Hope College

> Laurie Baron, copy editor
> Russell L. Gasero, production editor

Commission on History
> James Hart Brumm, M.Div., Blooming Grove, New York
> Lynn Japinga, Ph.D., Hope College, Holland, Michigan
> Mary L. Kansfield, M.A., New Brunswick, New Jersey
> Melody Meeter, M.Div., Brooklyn, New York
> Jesus Serrano, B.A., Norwalk, California
> Jeffrey Tyler, Ph.D., Hope College, Holland, Michigan

Contents

Illustrations

Editor's Foreword

Janet Sheeres has given us a moving, sympathetic, and exciting biography of one of the key figures in the Netherlands' *Afscheiding* of 1834 and the early development of the Christian Reformed Church. The book is meticulously researched, well written, and a treasure trove of information. The footnotes are not to be overlooked, as they might well be in the exciting flow of the story.

Sheeres's account of a man zealously committed to his understanding of God's Word and its implications for his life, even when it required the sacrifice of three secessions, challenges us in our contemporary commitment. At the same time, her sociological observations add interesting insights into the times. The incredibly high degree of mortality and short average life span is interspersed with such tidbits as the fact that in the *Afgescheiden* church in Donkerbroek, Friesland, the consistory members charged their pipes and tobacco to the church, or that at the time of Dominee Vander Werp's pastorate in Leeuwarden, the city of nineteen thousand had between thirty and forty houses of prostitution. Even the serious social ill of endemic alcoholism cannot prevent Sheeres from quoting an Englishman who in 1840 observed, "To the Dutch water was for washing and for sailing, but not for drinking."

The strange usage of *juffrouw* (a single woman) for the wives of seceder pastors, which in America became more generally used of married women and lasted into the twentieth century, also finds elucidation in Sheeres's pages.

In addition to being the biography of a Christian of high commitment (and secession), this book's appearance in the Historical

Series of the Reformed Church in America merits a word of explanation. Rapport between the Christian Reformed Church and the Reformed Church in America has grown gradually in recent decades. Beginning with the Dutch American Historical Association in 1963, whose initial purpose was sharing the archival materials of Calvin College and Seminary, Hope College and Western Seminary, through the decision in the eighties to publish curriculum materials jointly, cooperation has grown through joint services of worship, shared distribution facilities, and in the synods of 2005 the resolve to expedite shared ministry of Word and sacrament. While the Reformed Church in America has no periodical equivalent to the superb quality of *Origins*, it does have this historical series. Even as *Origins* has carried features concerning the Reformed Church, so we are pleased to include books of Christian Reformed origin in the Historical Series of the Reformed Church in America.

As the denominations draw closer together it is highly desirable that each understand the outlook of the other. To that end, a biography such as this is extremely valuable in helping members of the Reformed Church in America understand the history of the Christian Reformed Church. A comparison of this volume with that of Gerrit J. ten Zythoff, *Sources of Secession*, will give something of a different perspective. Just as Sheeres has helped us understand the life of the first minister of the Graafschaap Christian Reformed Church, so ten Zythoff can help members of the Christian Reformed Church see some of the same events from a perspective more common to that of the Reformed Church in America.

The level of commitment of Douwe Vander Werp to his understanding of the gospel must most certainly be respected. Even his vision of the church "based solidly on the Three Forms of Unity" (p. 149) is one that this editor can affirm. Having grown up believing, and later having taught the beauty of the theology of the Heidelberg Catechism effectively as a pastor and professor, as well as having espoused the Canons of Dort as being able to be understood as the high point of the Reformation, it is somthing of a surprise to find Vander Werp interpreting scripture in a way that puts me in a class with the unbelievers, the wicked, and those who live in darkness (p. 147). *Son of Secession* is a worthwhile and instructive story.

Donald J. Bruggink
General Editor
Historical Series of the Reformed Church in America

Preface

Douwe Johannes Vander Werp's life revolved around words—spoken and written. First as a schoolteacher, then as a lay preacher, later as an ordained minister, still later as a teacher again, this time of theology students, and finally as editor of a denominational biweekly newspaper.

Sometimes caring, sometimes caustic, but always cautionary, his words were meant to instruct his listeners of their need for salvation. How ironic then that this man should be struck with cancer of the mouth, silencing his flow of words.

During his years as an ordained minister, Vander Werp received forty-three calls (offers from churches to become their pastor). In the Netherlands he organized two churches; in America, ten churches in as many years.

In the Netherlands he was often a delegate to regional and national church meetings and served several times as clerk, for both synods and classes. From 1854 to 1864 he served as curator of the newly established theological school in Kampen. In 1859 he gathered and published all the synodical decisions of the *Christelijke Afgescheiden* Church. Along with two other ministers, he wrote *Apologie*, a document justifying the Secession of 1834.

In America he had a perfect attendance record at all the classis and general assembly (gathering of representatives of all the denominational congregations, later called synod) meetings from 1864 until 1875, when illness prevented him from attending. However, the greatest work he performed for the Christian Reformed denomination was passing on his knowledge, wisdom, and love for that church to the next generation of leaders, not out of selfish ambition or gain, but as a sacrificial service to the Lord of the church.

Vander Werp passed away April 1, 1876, in Muskegon, Michigan. Someone counted forty-two carriages in the funeral procession, indicating the high esteem in which he was held at the time of his passing.

I first "met" Vander Werp while researching my Sjaarda ancestors in Burum, Friesland. They were all dead, of course, Vander Werp as well as my ancestors. But in the second half of the 1800s they were very much alive and attended the *Christelijke Afgescheiden Kerk* in Burum, with Vander Werp as pastor and the Sjaardas as parishioners.

One of the Sjaardas, Derk, immigrated to America in 1853, settled in Muskegon, and became a member of the Muskegon True Dutch Reformed Church, where Vander Werp was his pastor from 1872 to 1876. So Vander Werp and the Sjaardas were acquainted with each other on both sides of the ocean.

Working at Calvin College in Grand Rapids, Michigan, I knew that one of the dormitories was named for Vander Werp and that he had trained young men before the denomination had a proper seminary. I thought if I found out more about Vander Werp's life, I might also find out more about the lives of my ancestors. I assumed it would be as simple as going to Calvin's Hekman Library and checking out the latest Vander Werp biography. Much to my disappointment, there was no Vander Werp biography on the library shelf.

In the Calvin Heritage Hall Archives I did find a biographical collection that contained several articles about Vander Werp and a limited collection of letters and pamphlets. The Internet was even less forthcoming, with only one reference to Vander Werp written in a paper about the *Afscheiding* in Smilde. From that paper, I gleaned that he had been the very first Christian School teacher in the Netherlands.

By then I was as intrigued with Vander Werp's history as with my ancestors' histories. I began searching through sources on the *Afscheiding* and in almost all of them I found references to Vander Werp. Gathering these pieces together, I had enough material to write a lengthy article for *Origins*, the magazine of Calvin's Archives. Having finished my research of Vander Werp, I hoped to resume researching my ancestors. Many people, however, after reading the *Origins* article about Vander Werp, encouraged me to enlarge on it and to write a full-length biography.

I realized that perhaps being from Burum, the Netherlands,

having been baptized in the same church of which Vander Werp was pastor, knowing the Dutch language, having crossed the ocean as an emigrant, being married to a minister and well acquainted with the Christian Reformed Church, I might just be the person to undertake this project. I hope you will enjoy "meeting" Douwe Vander Werp as much as I have.

Acknowledgments

No matter what we endeavor, we all benefit and build on the efforts of others. One of those "others" for me certainly was someone I have never met, but to whom I am deeply indebted—the late Dr. Jan Wesseling (1912 - 1989) of the Netherlands. Dr. Wesseling spent much of his life pouring over the minutes of the *Afgescheiden* churches of the Netherlands for his books on the subject. The books dealing with the *Afscheiding* in the northern provinces were especially relevant to my research on the life of Douwe Vander Werp.

Two initial readers who encouraged me to continue were Dr. Gerlof Homan, emeritus professor of history at the University of Illinois, and Gordon De Young, retired editor of Baker Book House. Their encouragement as well as that of the members of the Christian Reformed Church Historical Committee kept me going.

I would also like to acknowledge the staff of the Calvin College Archives—Dr. Richard Harms, Wendy Blankespoor, Hendrina Van Spronsen, and Boukje Leegwater—for their patience whenever I asked to look at one more collection in my search for one more fact. I am also indebted to the four anonymous members of the Origins Studies in Dutch-American History board of editors for reading the manuscript and offering valuable insights and corrections, as well as to Origins Studies in Dutch-American History through whose generous assistance the publication of this volume has been made possible.

And where would an author be without an excellent copy editor and layout artist—thank you Laurie Baron and Russell Gasero.

Finally, my husband, Gerrit W. Sheeres, emeritus minister of the Christian Reformed Church, deserves my deepest gratitude for his unfailing encouragement, solid suggestions, and his thorough knowledge of the Christian Reformed Church.

Introduction

Douwe Vander Werp's life can be understood best against the backdrop of the religious struggles of his time.

After the Reformation became a fact at the end of the sixteenth century, a majority of the members of the Reformed Church in the United Provinces of the Netherlands held to the doctrines of John Calvin. But the question arose, to what extent could a church prescribe and expect adherence to his or the doctrines of other leaders. Jacobus Arminius (1559-1609) and Franciscus Gomarus ((1563 – 1641), two theologians at the University of Leiden, struggled especially with the question of predestination.

This debate became a national conflict. The followers of Gomarus wanted to solve it by instituting the doctrine of predestination (God chooses his elect) as binding on all church members. Arminius argued that God gave humans a free will to accept or reject God's atoning work through Jesus. Arminius's followers, called the *Remonstranten* (those who disagreed and remonstrated), were also in favor of a certain amount of political independence for each province and peace with Spain, while Gomarus's followers, called the *Contraremonstranten*, promoted a strong central rule in the person of the *Stadhouder* and the continuation of the war for independence from Spain.[1]

To resolve this conflict, Prince Maurice, son of William of Orange, the *Stadhouder* of five provinces at the time, initiated a national synod at Dordrecht in 1618. In doing so he came in conflict with another

---

[1]   From 1568 to 1648 the Dutch fought an eighty-year war to gain their independence from Spain, broken by a twelve-year cease-fire (1609-1621), during which years the Synod of Dort was held.

powerful statesman, Johan van Oldebarneveld (1547-1619), Grand Pensionary of the influential province of Holland, who pushed for a truce with Spain and urged the Reformed Church to accept the teaching of the *Remonstranten*. Maurice replaced many of the pro-Arminian local politicians with anti-Arminian politicians and arrested Oldebarneveld on charges of treason. In 1619, the States General ordered the execution of Oldebarneveld; in the same year the Synod of Dort accepted the doctrines of the *Contraremonstranten* (the party of the Gomarists). The ensuing ecclesiastical body became known as the Reformed Church, the only church officially acknowledged by the state.

The States General, the government of the Republic, oversaw the activities of the church and often interfered when it felt the need to keep the peace. The state paid the salaries of the Reformed Church clergy and controlled the curriculum of the state universities in Leiden, Groningen, and Franeker, insuring that the ministers trained in these universities would promote the welfare of the state.[2] In fact, all ministers needed the consent of the government before being eligible for a call. While often referred to as the state church of the Netherlands, the Reformed Church was not actually a state church since membership was not guaranteed by citizenship. Membership was tied to specific requirements and official acceptance of church doctrines.[3] However, it certainly was *the* public church for all of the Netherlands—the church in which religion and state aided and abetted each other.

This Reformed Church adopted three documents as its doctrinal standards: the Heidelberg Catechism, the Canons of Dort, and the Belgic Confession.[4] Anyone wishing to become a minister in this church was required to sign a form of subscription stating that he believed these three forms to be in agreement with the Word of God. The Synod of Dort also adopted a church order outlining how churches were to be governed. From that synod in 1618 until 1816, when King William I convened another national synod, all synods were held at the provincial

---

[2]   D. H. Kromminga, *The Christian Reformed Tradition, From the Reformation to the Present* (Grand Rapids: Eerdmans, 1943), 41-46.

[3]   The official name of this denomination was *De Gereformeerde Kerk in de Verenigde Nederlanden*. In 1816 King William I changed the name to *De Hervormde Kerk in het Koninkrijk der Nederlanden*. To avoid confusion, I will use the term Reformed Church for both.

[4]   The Heidelberg Catechism was coauthored by Zacharius Ursinus and Caspar Olevianus in1563; the Canons of Dort was the result of the Synod of Dort 1618-19; the Belgic Confession was written by Guido de Brès in 1561.

level and dealt with regional problems and concerns, always adhering to the church order established by the Synod of Dort.

Since the Reformation, most non-Catholic Dutch believers have belonged to the Reformed Church. By the end of the eighteenth century, however, many of the clergy and leading members of society had strayed from the doctrinal standards set forth by the Synod of Dort and espoused more "enlightened" views. Fearing dissension, governmental oversight suppressed much frank and open theological dialogue, adding to the malaise of the church. Finally, the government's refusal to convene national synods for two centuries weakened the spiritual backbone of the corporate body severely.[5]

The 1795 French invasion of the Netherlands resulted in the formation of the Batavian Republic and the separation of church and state. When the French retreated in 1815, the Dutch proclaimed Prince William, scion of the Dutch House of Orange, as their first king, William I. The new king decided in 1816 to make the Reformed Church the official state church of the Netherlands, much like the Anglican Church in England and the Lutheran churches in Scandinavia. Rather furtively, he convened a national synod, choosing the delegates himself.[6] A new set of church regulations was enacted that included a subtle change in wording in the form of subscription. The word *quia* (*because* these teachings are in agreement with God's Word) was changed to *quatenus* (*in so far as* these teachings are in agreement with God's Word), so that those who did not believe fully in these doctrines were given more liberty to sign.[7] This word change would have great repercussions several decades later. Because many pastors had embraced the Enlightenment, their sermons reflected these views. The Synod of Dort's strong stand on humanity's sinful state and need for redemption was no longer thought to be reasonable. These more liberal-minded pastors considered Jesus a great teacher and example, and Bible stories were seen as tools to help people live better lives. *"Niet de leer, maar de Heer"* ("Not doctrines, but the Lord") became their slogan.

This reorganization of the Reformed Church by William I and the liberal theological preaching troubled many conservative Christians. However, since voting rights were vested in wealthier members who

---

[5] Kromminga, *Reformed Tradition*, 42.

[6] H. Algra, *Het wonder van de negentiende eeuw: Van vrije kerken en kleine luyden*, 4th ed. (Franeker: Wever, 1976), 63-64.

[7] J. C. van der Does, *De Afscheiding in haar wording en beginperiode*, 2nd ed. (Delft: Meinema, 1934), 21.

often sided with the government, poorer members had no voice, neither in their civil nor in their church government. Therefore, instead of attending church, they met in each other's homes. These cells, or *conventicles*, had a long tradition going back to the Reformation, but now took on a new and more fervent character.[8] The government frowned upon these groups since they drained members away from the state church. They also were considered to be in opposition to the established order. Not only the government, but the well-to-do and leading citizens of places such as Vander Werp's home town of Uithuizen looked down on those who withdrew from the official church and considered them rabble.

In October 1834, under the leadership of the orthodox minister Hendrik De Cock, the majority of the congregation at Ulrum, a small town in the northern province of Groningen, officially seceded from the Reformed Church. All over the Netherlands, those meeting in conventicles joined the secession movement by forming congregations, and a new denomination was born. According to Algra, the conventicles were the foundation of the *Afgescheiden* churches.[9] However, like all births, this one was not without pain. King William I, hoping to crush what he considered insurrection, ordered stiff measures against the Seceders. For sixteen years, until his abdication in 1840, the Seceders suffered persecution from civil authorities as well as from employers and fellow citizens. Douwe Vander Werp's story is one of hundreds of stories about people who stayed true to their convictions in spite of the consequences.

For those interested in a more detailed account of the *Afscheiding* in the English language, I suggest *Sources of Secession, The Netherlands Hervormde Kerk on the Eve of the Dutch Immigration to the Midwest*, by G. J. ten Zythoff, (Eerdmans, 1987); *The Christian Reformed Tradition, from the Reformation to the Present*, by D. H. Kromminga (Eerdmans, 1943); and *Our Family Album: The Unfinished Story of the Christian Reformed Church*, by James C. Schaap (CRC Publications, 1998).

[8]   C. Van Rijswijk, *De Poorten Sions bemind boven alle woningen Jacobs* (Zwijndrecht, Van den Berg, 1983), 20, 26-27, 148-54. Martin Bucer (1491-1551), one of the leaders of the German Reformation, believed that it was the task of Christians to admonish and encourage each other. This was best done in small groups. The practice took hold in the Netherlands, and by 1629 the Reformed Church controlled the conventicles and gave the movement guidance and structure by issuing rules. By the time of the *Afscheiding*, however, these conventicles, dissatisfied as they were with the Reformed Church's liberal teachings, met without church supervision, often appointing their own lay preachers.

[9]   Algra, *Wonder*, 100. In a matter of five years there were 150 *Afgescheiden* congregations. Most of these congregations were organized from existing conventicles.

CHAPTER 1

Family and Church

The marriage of Catharina Huizenga and Johannes Vander Werp on June 10, 1810, may well have raised a few eyebrows in Uithuizen, a small town in the province of Groningen. Catharina's parents were respected residents of the town. Her mother was a midwife and her father a shipping broker and inspector, while Johannes was merely a *beurtschipper*.[1] In spite of their importance to the national economy, *beurtschippers* were often looked down upon as being a lower class of people, who—like gypsies—were always on the go, without a permanent home to call their own, except *het roefje,* or cabin, on their boat

To save the cost of a house, Dutch *schipper* families lived on board. These families formed a close-knit society of their own and usually married within their own group. Brokers, on the other hand, kept track of products needing to be shipped, from where to where, and made a good living from the shipping trade. Even so, in spite of class differences, Johannes and Catharina had fallen in love; no amount of parental advice from either side mattered. After their wedding, Catharina left her parents' comfortable home on the Boterdiep quay and joined Johannes in the cramped quarters of his boat.

---

[1]   *Beurtschippers* were bargemen assigned to regular routes at regular times. Their boats, routes, and cargoes were monitored carefully by shipping brokers who also acted as inspectors. In the Netherlands, until the middle of the twentieth century, most goods were transported by boats navigated by *beurtschippers*. For a careful study of *beurtschippers*, see Hylke Speerstra, *De voorbije vloot: Verhalen en herinneringen van de laatste echte schippers* (Amsterdam: Contact, 2001).

1

View of Groningen city harbor

Ten months later, on April 13, 1811, Catherine gave birth to a son while moored in their home port, the city of Groningen. The child, Douwe, was named after his paternal grandfather, Douwe Vander Werp, who as a young man had been a soldier stationed in Leeuwarden, in the province of Friesland. The name *Douwe* is the Frisian version of the Latin Dominicus.[2] Rather fittingly, the term *dominee*, the Dutch term for minister, comes from the same root word. *Werp* is an old Frisian word for *kwelder*, or land situated outside the dikes that had silted in but did not flood over with normal tides. Those working this land were called *kwelder* farmers and were given the name "from the *kwelder*," or "*van de werp*." Perhaps one of Vander Werp's forefathers had been such a farmer.

From his birth until age six, Douwe lived on board ship with his parents. When he was four his brother, Jan Hendrik, was born. Although their play area on board was rather limited, there were always new sights to see as the boat made its regular journey between Groningen and Uithuizen. In Uithuizen they had the run of their grandparents' stately home on the quay; in Groningen they enjoyed the hustle and bustle of city life; and in between, there were the farms and villages and other boats to keep them entertained. Both brothers would weather many storms, but the bond formed between them in their childhood would last a lifetime.

[2]   A. Huizinga, ed., *Encyclopedie van voornamen* (Amsterdam: Strengholt, n.d.), 69.

Marketplace, city of Groningen

When *schipper* children reached school age, it was customary to board them with relatives or friends during the school week. Douwe entered the public school in Uithuizen in 1817 and began boarding with his Huizenga grandparents. This lasted only one year, because in 1818 grandmother Huizenga passed away. In that same year, Johannes and Catharina left their boat to settle in Uithuizen. Catharina's father was getting on in years, and Catharina may have felt it her duty to look after him. He passed away five years later, in 1823. Jan Hendrik, her second child, was reaching school age and would also have to be boarded out if they stayed on the boat. Then, too, in November 1818, Catharina gave birth to their third son, Hendrik, and she may not have wanted to raise another child on the boat. The sale of the boat provided Johannes with enough funds to establish himself as a tinsmith. They settled in a house on Zuiderstraat, near the Boterdiep quay in Uithuizen.[3]

Uithuizen, a small, prosperous community in the northern part of the province, provided a secure and stable place for Douwe's next phase of growing up. The town was no sleepy backwater—already in 1670 daily canal boat service connected Uithuizen to the city of Groningen. A person could leave Uithuizen early in the morning, arrive

---

[3]   B. De Groot, "Douwe Johannes van der Werp, 1811-1876: Een Cocksiaan van het eerste uur," *Jaarboek voor de geschiedenis van de Gereformeerde Kerken in Nederland,* no. 3, D. Th. Kuiper, ed. (Kampen: Kok, n.d.), 41.

Uithuizen, mail and
telegraph office

in Groningen in time for the cattle markets, and return home the same evening. Any purchases were easily shipped home with a *beurtschipper*.

While much of the Netherlands suffered economically under the French annexation (1795-1813), the province of Groningen prospered. The French blockade of Great Britain assured that no grain could leave that country—to the advantage of grain farmers in Groningen. Moreover, the citizens of the province engaged in lucrative smuggling, adding to the region's flourishing economy.[4] Uithuizen's annual cattle and horse market, which drew many from the surrounding countryside, also added to the town's income. These market days brought in entertainment as well—merry-go-rounds, barrel organs, and colorful stalls of the out-of-town vendors—delighting young and old.

---

[4]   P. Steringa, *Nederlanders op reis in Amerika 1812-1860: Reisverhalen als bron voor negentiende-eeuwse mentaliteit*, Utrechtse Historische Cahiers, 20 vols. (Utrecht: Universiteit Utrecht, 1999), 1, 25. During the French annexation of the Netherlands (1810-1813), France put an embargo on trade with its enemy, Great Britain, and only allowed trade with countries on the European continent. The Groninger port of Delfzijl therefore was allowed to remain open to trade with Germany, and a large scale smuggling operation ensued from this port.

Uithuizen harbor
scene

    With his mother occupied by the care of his younger siblings and his newly widowed grandfather, and his father busily engaged in building up his tinsmith business, Douwe was left on his own to explore the town, after years of having been confined to the boat. Whether watching the town's many craftsmen—carpenters, tinsmiths, shoemakers, etc.—at work in their shops, or spending time watching boats being loaded and unloaded along the Boterdiep, Douwe and his friends had plenty to keep themselves amused and out of trouble after school. For a youngster like Douwe, who was not caught in the cycle of poverty that required going to work at an early age, these were happy and carefree years.

    The church also played a large role in the life of the family. Of the town's three churches— Reformed, Roman Catholic, and Mennonite— the Reformed Church was the most influential. When the Vander Werps settled in Uithuizen, Johannes joined and Catharina rejoined the Reformed Church, the church in which she had grown up, and in which she and Johannes had been married. The congregation genuinely loved their pastor, Wilhelmus Janssonius, who had led the congregation at Uithuizen for as long as Catharina could remember. He came in 1792 and stayed until his death in 1825 at age sixty.[5] Nevertheless, while all seemed peaceful on the outside, small tears of discontent were showing up in this otherwise well-woven fabric. Without knowing it, Uithuizen was only a decade away from a full-fledged church split, with young Douwe right in the thick of it.

---

[5]   He was followed by J. Muntendam from 1827 to 1829, and by Laurentius Meijer-Brouwer from 1829 to 1858.

CHAPTER 2

School and Storm

It never occurred to Catharina, when she brought Douwe to school for the first time, that her influence over him would be replaced by that of others, whose religious convictions she did not share. Like most parents, she hoped that he would apply himself to his studies and eventually make something of himself. Having grown up in Uithuizen, Catharina had attended the same school at a time when the Reformed Church in Uithuizen, as elsewhere in the Netherlands, had been in firm control of educating the nation's youth.

This state of affairs ended in 1795, when France invaded the Netherlands, resulting in the formation of the Batavian Republic, which in turn separated church and state, whereby the Reformed Church lost its influence over public education. In 1806 a new national public school law went into effect, stating that all public education was to be strictly neutral with no one religious persuasion dominating. Teaching the Heidelberg Catechism or other Reformed creeds offensive to Roman Catholics, Mennonites, and Jews was no longer allowed. The primary task of the new educational system was to instill in the pupil good citizenship, patriotism, Christian virtues, and, after 1813, a love for the Dutch Royal House. The school day opened and closed with a proper and respectful prayer and the singing of an appropriate song.

The Reformed Church had given its stamp of approval when the law was passed, and Johannes and Catharina agreed with the church's stand. However, the passing of this new public education law did not mean that the bond between church and school was immediately broken. On the contrary, very little changed at first—the spiritual climate in the schools remained, on the whole, Christian.[1] The fact that little changed as to the religious content in the school in Uithuizen was largely due to the school's headmaster, Hidde Lucas Wessels.

Wessels, an excellent teacher and proponent of these new educational methods, used incentives such as praise and rewards, instead of scolding and physical punishment, to instill good behavior. He had published several books on mathematics and was, in general, highly regarded.[2] Nevertheless, Wessels lamented the fact that the new school law neutralized Christianity. His refusal to consider the views of others in this matter did not endear him to the school supervisor. A member of the Reformed Church, he was not pleased with the current religious state of affairs of his church either. After Laurentius Meijer-Brouwer became the pastor in Uithuizen in 1829, Wessels published pamphlets criticizing his pastor's preaching and theology. His strongly conservative spiritual leaning no doubt, influenced his pupils— including Douwe. Perhaps it was Douwe's respect and admiration for his teacher that led to his decision to become a teacher as well.

During Douwe's years at the school, a large and attractive new building replaced the existing one. This building consisted of two classrooms, separated by glass partitions so that the headmaster could easily oversee the activities in each room. New and improved school buildings were going up around the country, and the government urged that all children attend school. That created a need for bright and energetic teachers. Douwe's goal to continue his education and become a full-fledged teacher should have been attainable. That is, until disaster struck the Netherlands.

Two months before his fourteenth birthday, a natural catastrophe swept over Holland. The unseasonably warm weather on the first day of February 1825 may have been welcome, but not what followed.

---

[1]   Alje Bolt, *Geschiedenis van Uithuizen van de middeleeuwen tot en met 31 december 1978* (Uithuizen: Bakker, 1982), 98.

[2]   J. Wesseling, *De Afscheiding van 1834 in Groningerland*, 3 vols. (Groningen, De Vuurbaak, 1972-1978), 3: 30. H. L. Wessels came to Uithuizen from Oude Pekela April 22, 1810. He stayed until 1847. See also J. Reinsma, *Scholen en Schoolmeesters onder Willem I en II* (Den Haag, N.V. Voorheen Van Keulen Periodieken, 1965), 106. The national school supervisor, Wijnbeek, described Wessels as having exaggerated emotions, being a fanatical follower of De Cock, and as someone who spent a great deal of his time writing tracts against his Reformed pastor.

By afternoon of the next day the wind, blowing from the southwest, increased steadily in intensity. After three days of torrential rains, the wind shifted and began raging in strong gusts from the northwest. Roaring on for days, alternating with snow, rain, sleet, and lightning, the storm broke dikes and levees, inundating whole coastal plains as well as inland areas. Nationwide, the flood of 1825 went into the record books as one of the most damaging in human lives and property loss. Unlike in other provinces—Friesland and Overijssel together counted 350 deaths—no human lives were lost in the province of Groningen, but the province sustained much damage as water flooded low-lying areas, especially along the Eems and Dollard Rivers and north of Zoutkamp. Coastal areas in the north of the province were affected as well.

The chilling sounds of church bells tolling over the raging storm, the sight of fearful people streaming into town from low-lying areas, the bleating of cattle being led to higher ground, and the threat of water coming ever nearer perhaps also shook Douwe's sense of security. Perhaps these fearful days were the beginning of his religious conversion. Had God not punished evil people with floods before? God's awesome power over nature had to be acknowledged one way or another. More enlightened people reasoned that this was an act of nature, albeit a very destructive one. But those meeting in conventicles and unhappy with the church's teaching knew better—God was punishing the country. At school, Wessels instructed his pupils accordingly. One could expect soldiers and old people to die, but floods, disease, and death were no respecters of age, he lectured them. Even children needed to repent and be saved.[3]

Mr. Wessels's concern for his pupils' eternal salvation was not without a basis in reality. Three of his own children had died while very young.[4] During the years Douwe attended grade school, there were always one, two, or more of his classmates who passed away. In 1817, out of the total of twenty-five deaths in Uithuizen, nine were children under the age of thirteen; this ratio of children's deaths to adults stayed consistent until 1824 when out of forty-seven deaths, twenty-one (almost half) were children under the age of fourteen.[5] It is highly

3   Reinsma, *Scholen en Schoolmeesters,* 106.
4   Lucas, age 7, 1816; Johannes, age 5, 1817; Titia, 4 months in 1826. From: Civil Registry, Deaths, Uithuizen, the Netherlands, Family History Library, Salt Lake City, Utah, International Film #109,603.
5   Ibid. In 1817, out of the total of 25 deaths for Uithuizen, 9 were children under the age of 13; in 1818, out of 29 deaths, 8 were children under the age of 13; in 1819, out

unlikely that a man like Wessels, who took the scriptures seriously, would neglect the spiritual care of his charges; instead, it is more likely that he would admonish them to accept Jesus as their Savior, even in their young lives, lest they perish eternally.

The years immediately after the flood were as disastrous as the flood itself. The weather continued wet and cold, and the number of deaths due to disease increased far above average death rates. In 1826 the number of deaths in Uithuizen spiked to seventy-two, of which thirty-three were children under the age of thirteen.[6] Crops failed and the plight of the farmers had a direct effect on the small shopkeepers in town. The flood had only exacerbated a stagnant economy that had begun in the 1820s with foreign wheat driving down grain prices. The economic downturn also hurt his father's tinsmith business, which may have been the reason why Douwe did not attend a teacher's training school. His formal grade school years were completed by 1826, and without additional schooling, he was destined to become either a *beurtschipper*, like his brother Jan Hendrik, or a tradesman, like his father. But Wessels had seen potential in Douwe, and, knowing that the new school law opened up positions to anyone who could pass the examination, offered to tutor him after hours. Four years later, at age eighteen, Douwe passed the third rank examination that qualified him as an assistant teacher.[7] Now only one civic obligation stood between him and the start of his teaching career—the military draft. The Dutch used a lottery system, and once a year the nation's eighteen-year-olds

---

of 31 deaths, 7 were children; in 1820, out of 25 deaths, 9 were children; in 1821, out of 38 deaths, 7 were children under the age of 13; in 1822, out of 24 deaths, 6 were children under the age of 13; in 1823, out of 42 deaths 19 were children under the age of 13; in 1824, out of 47 deaths, 21 (almost half) were children under the age of 14; and in 1825, out of 57 deaths, 15 were children.

[6] Ibid.

[7] E. P. Booy and P. Th. F. M. Boekholt, *Geschiedenis van de school in Nederland: vanaf de middeleeuwen tot aan de huidige tijd* (Assen: Van Gorcum, 1987), 110, 112. To achieve a fourth (the lowest) rank, a teacher had to be proficient in reading, writing and arithmetic. For the third rank, besides the three aforementioned skills, he also had to know how to use fractions in arithmetic and the basics of the Dutch language. These two ranks only allowed a person to be an assistant teacher. To be in charge of a school one had to achieve at least the second rank. For the second rank, besides knowledge required of the third and fourth, was added knowledge of geography, history, and grammar. And to obtain the first rank, a teacher had to be proficient in all the subjects mentioned in the first three levels as well as natural science and mathematics.

had to appear before municipal officials to draw lots. Fortunately for Douwe, he drew a number which excused him from service. Shortly thereafter, he found a teaching position in Houwerzijl, a small village in the province of Groningen, where the aging and ailing teacher, Wieko Pietersen, needed an assistant.[8]

How pleased Johannes and Catharine must have been to have their oldest son become a respected schoolteacher, not knowing that in a few short years his actions would raise more eyebrows in Uithuizen than their marriage had ever done.

---

[8] J. S. van Weerden, *Spanningen en konflikten: Verkenningen rondom de Afscheiding van 1834* (Groningen: Sasland, 1967), 90. In 1797, Wieko Pietersen came from Wijbelsum, East Friesland to teach in Houwerzijl. He also served as custodian and *voorzanger* for the congregation of Niekerk to which Houwerzijl belonged. He had contact with H. De Cock as early as 1831. See also Wesseling, *Groningerland*, 2: 101. Vander Werp began his teaching career sometime in 1829. The exact day and month are unknown.

CHAPTER 3

Douwe and De Cock

Pietersen was well pleased with his protégé. Vander Werp, full of youthful enthusiasm, taught the children, endeared himself to the parents, and improved the curriculum. Since he boarded with the Pietersens, Douwe made himself useful around the house as well. When Pietersen approached Vander Werp about taking over his duties as *voorzanger* at the Niekerk church, the latter consented.[1] The people of Houwerzijl belonged to the parish of Niekerk, so it was only natural that this was where he would attend church services. He found that he enjoyed being in front of the congregation and leading them in the singing and scripture reading. Pietersen seemed glad not to have to attend services in Niekerk anymore—he was, he told Vander Werp more than once, not happy with his pastor's liberal preaching.[2] Conversely, Niekerk's pastor was not pleased with Pietersen's conservative teaching. Although the pastor's children belonged to the Houwerzijl school district, he taught them at home.

A year or two later, when rumors were floating around that Ulrum's new pastor, Hendrik De Cock, was preaching more doctrinally sound sermons, many people gladly walked long distances to hear him.

---

[1] The *voorzanger* led the congregation in singing, read scripture, and made announcements. This duty was often assigned to the school teacher.

[2] Wesseling, *Groningerland*, 2: 101. J. van der Helm of Niekerk, Pietersen's pastor, was not happy with the latter's wife's association with De Cock, and in protest did not send his children to Pietersen's school in Houwerzijl.

So also, Pietersen's wife. Sunday evenings she would tell her husband and Vander Werp all about the fiery preacher in Ulrum.

In their discussions about De Cock they may well have noted that until he came to Ulrum, De Cock had never studied the writings of John Calvin, that he had not read the Canons of Dort until some of his parishioners encouraged him to do so, and that he was beginning to understand what being *reformed* really meant. How grateful they must have been to know that God was providing a true shepherd to lead them during this troubled time in their nation's history.

One of those troubles was the war with Belgium that had broken out in 1830. People were anxious about the standoff, unhappy with the military draft and the military tax levied to pay for the war. In the province of Groningen the war had also deprived the grain farmers of the Belgium market. The farmers in the municipality of Leens protested so vigorously against the government that soldiers were called in to keep the peace.

In contrast to his more liberal colleagues, De Cock did not hesitate to use the war as a sign of God's wrath on an apostate nation. When at the same time a cholera epidemic swept through the Netherlands

---

Hendrik De Cock

Son of Tjaarda De Cock and Jantje De Boer, Hendrik was born April 12, 1801, in Veendam, the Province of Groningen. Shortly after his birth the family moved to Wildervank, where his father became mayor. Hendrik studied theology at the University of Groningen. On February 14, 1824, he married Frouwe Venema. They had five children. One month later, on the seventh of March, he preached his inaugural sermon in Eppenhuizen, Province of Groningen. He labored there until November 1827 when he went to Noordlaren, and two years later, November 29, 1829, was installed by his good friend P. Hofstede De Groot at Ulrum. Even though he had received a theology degree from the University of Groningen, De Cock was not familiar with Calvin's Institutes or the Canons of Dordrecht. This changed when one of his Ulrum parishioners, Klaas Pieters Kuipenga, challenged De Cock about the doctrine of salvation by grace, and De Cock began to study seriously the Reformed doctrines.

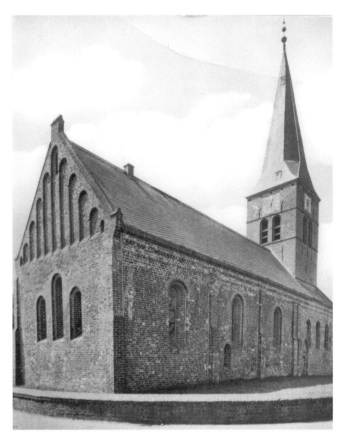

Ulrum Dutch Reformed Church

claiming the lives of many, De Cock saw this epidemic as yet another scourge of God.[3]

Unlike outbreaks of smallpox, measles, and typhoid fever, which occurred regularly in the Netherlands, cholera was unknown. It had originated in India, entered the European continent via Russia through Constantinople and moved north. Early in 1832, Dutch newspapers reported that it had reached Paris and that refugees fleeing Paris had brought it to Belgium. In order to stave off the disease, the Dutch government initiated counter-measures, including that of closing the border with Belgium. However, they did not close off their seaports, and the disease entered the country at Scheveningen via a fishing vessel late in June. By August it had reached the city of Amsterdam. The first

[3]   Marita Mathijsen, *De Gemaskerde Eeuw* (Amsterdam: Querido, 2002), 113-19.

wave of the epidemic killed more than ten thousand people, causing large-scale fear and panic.[4]

Coming hard on the heels of the 1825 flood and the exceedingly poor economic years that followed, warnings from the Ulrum pulpit were received favorably by those who had said that God was punishing the nation. De Cock's services were attended by more and more of those who preferred this style of preaching.[5]

Pietersen invited De Cock to his home in Houwerzijl. His wife was ill, he told De Cock, and could not come to his church. Would he please come and visit her? De Cock agreed. At these visits Vander Werp was also present. De Cock's formal education far outdistanced that of Vander Werp, yet, in spite of the difference, he recognized in the young teacher a burning spirit to serve the Lord. Vander Werp in turn recognized in De Cock a man of God. Soon De Cock's cause became Vander Werp's cause. When De Cock complained one day about his mountains of paperwork, Vander Werp offered his writing services. Fine penmanship was a skill much admired and in demand in a time when writing meant goose-quill pens and ink, blotters and inkwells. De Cock accepted Vander Werp's help gladly, and the bond formed between the two men would last until De Cock's death.

De Cock's writing load had increased in direct proportion to his popularity, and to the opposition he received, the latter coming especially from his fellow clergymen. One of them, his friend and classmate at the theological school in Groningen, Petrus Hofstede de Groot, had been pastor in Ulrum before De Cock. The two began to correspond regarding their views on theology, with De Groot warning De Cock about preaching such fearful sermons to the congregation that he had once loved.

Vander Werp, emboldened by De Cock, also entered the writing fray. In 1832 he wrote to his parents,

> Yes, dear parents, may the Almighty also teach you to recognize
> your frailty and bring you to the kingdom of His Son, by whose

---

4   Gerrit J. tenZythoff, *Sources of Secession: The Netherlands Hervormde Kerk on the Eve of the Dutch Immigration to the Midwest* (Grand Rapids: Eerdmans, 1987), 116.

5   G. Keizer, *De Afscheiding van 1834: Haar aanleiding naar authentieke brieven* (Kampen: Kok, 1934), 185. Due to the cholera epidemic, comets, and damaging fall storms, King William I initiated a special prayer service December 2, 1832. Many sermons preached and in print called these disasters the "rod of God over the Netherlands" and called for national repentance. See also tenZythoff, *Sources of Secession*, 116-17.

stripes we are healed. Oh! That He would open your eyes so that you might see how full of festering sores and boils you are, which you are not able to see now. Oh, that you might also taste of the Lord's goodness. Oh, that you might also be among his elect, and belong to his children, Yes, to his dear ones. Oh, may the Lord give you some of the crumbs of the living bread of life and some drops of that living water of His Grace.[6]

No doubt some of his words were meant to admonish his parents about their church attendance since their pastor, Laurentius Meijer-Brouwer, warned his parishioners against the ultra orthodox teachings of De Cock.[7] From Uithuizen, too, dissidents had been traveling to Ulrum, but Vander Werp's parents were not among them. As lifetime members of the Reformed Church, they considered themselves good Christians and were not happy with the unrest created by some, nor with the rumors that their son was working actively for and with De Cock. They wrote to him to consider his actions seriously. Vander Werp defended his position in a letter, dated July 30, 1832.[8]

Dearly Beloved Father and Mother! Since I promised in my previous letter of June 30, that, if the Lord wills it, I would soon write a follow-up letter, so I now feel myself to be strong and bold to begin and hope that God's Holy Spirit will give me further strength and be near me. The reason I write to you is because there are some of the brothers and sisters in the Lord here who distrust the state of my soul and are making an unjust judgment regarding me, something which is not their right to do because the Lord will repay each according to their works and everyone's work shall be brought into judgment. Please, dear ones, do not judge me either. Because I know and the Lord knows what He has put in my heart and has allowed me to experience. To prevent judgment or to take it away if it should come up, or who knows, already has come up, but I can hardly think that of you, I hope that the Lord will prevent it. Jesus said, "Judge not so that you will not be judged, because with whatever judgment you judge, you will be judged yourself." Still I carry these wrong accusations patiently

6   De Wachter, July 8, 1969.
7   Laurentius Meijer-Brouwer (1786-1872) was born in Oudwoude, Friesland. He served several churches before moving to Uithuizen in 1829, staying until his retirement in 1858. He passed away in Appingedam in 1872.
8   De Wachter, June 10, 1969.

and with resignation and I look toward the recompense which does not come from people, but through faith in the precious blood of Jesus Christ, which He, to satisfy God's righteousness, shed on Golgotha and by which I will be made righteous and in which I find forgiveness of my sins through the blood of Grace.

Later on in the same long letter, Vander Werp explained to his parents how he bore the accusations.

As to the accusations, to return to these, I follow my great Example, Jesus, the Head of his church, who, when he stood before Pilate, and although he was accused of many things, was patient and silent. Yes, even before the judgment seat of Pilate, so also I will be silent before all my accusers. Yes, Pilate, himself was surprised and said, "There are many witnesses leveling accusations against you, do you not want to answer these?" Still Jesus remained silent. Then Pilate said heatedly, "Why don't you answer me, don't you know that I have the power to release you and the power to crucify you?" Then it was time for Jesus to answer him and to state his case before Pilate, to make him feel powerless: "You would not have any power over me if it had not been given to you from above," Jesus said to him, "Don't you understand that I can ask my Father and he can send twelve legions of angels to deliver me?" Yes, dear ones, so I will also be strengthened through God's Spirit if it is for the honor of God's name and for the advancement of Jesus' pure doctrine and church. Even if I have to appear before kings and rulers and governors. Yes, this is my daily prayer, that the Lord, in my time, now that the doctrine of the Gospel is scorned and ridiculed, will give me courage and strength to come out more openly for the righteous belief in my Savior, whether it be to rich or poor, to important or inconsequential, and that the Holy Spirit may give me the words to speak in that hour, Yes, and that strength will be given me also in such a time so that I will not be hindered by fear of people.

This letter gives us a glimpse into Vander Werp's religious thoughts. He speaks of "what the Lord has allowed me to experience." The conversion experience was a vital test of the spirituality of the Seceders—without having experienced one's own sinfulness, there was no hope of deliverance, because one would not search for a Savior. This idea of knowing one's sins was addressed in one of the first questions of the Heidelberg Catechism, "What must I know to be saved?" Answer: "How great my sins and misery are." From the letter to his parents it is clear that young Vander Werp felt that his parents had not yet been convicted of their "sins and misery."

As more and more people came to the parsonage in Ulrum to seek advice, Vander Werp began spending more and more time at De Cock's side. Now it was Vander Werp who informed the Pietersens about the news from Ulrum. He told them how Luitsen Dijkstra, a simple peat farmer, had walked for nine hours from Smilde, in the province of Drenthe, just to meet with De Cock. How the people in the province of Drenthe were meeting in small groups instead of going to their parish churches. How De Cock was dealing with the rift between him and his fellow clergymen.

This rift widened even more when Meijer-Brouwer published two sermons in 1833 titled, *Necessary Warnings* and *Beneficial Advice to my Congregation*, in which he warned the members of his congregation against preachers like De Cock who preached humanity's total helplessness (with respect to the doctrine of election, a favorite teaching of the conservatives, but not of the enlightened). Soon after followed a publication by the Reverend Gerard Benthem-Reddingius of Assen, *Letters regarding the current divisions in the Church*, in which he spoke out against those meeting in conventicles.[9]

Several times a week, Vander Werp walked the five kilometers between Houwerzijl and Ulrum to assist De Cock. He used the solitary time to formulate his thoughts on the charges brought against De Cock. He chafed under the unfairness of the accusations leveled against his friend. When, for instance, De Cock confronted Meijer-Brouwer about the publications written by the latter against him, Meijer-Brouwer challenged De Cock to refute them publicly. Vander Werp wondered how and when De Cock would defend himself against his adversaries.

A clash came even sooner than anyone could have foreseen.

---

[9] Gerard Benthem-Reddingius (1774-1844) was pastor of the Reformed Church in Assen, clerk of the Provincial Synod of Drenthe, a member of the committee that wrote the new church order for the Reformed Church in 1816, and a fierce opponent of the Seceders.

CHAPTER 4

Charges and Countercharges

One Sunday in April 1833, after having heard De Cock preach on the three marks of the true church, Arend Schoonoort of Uithuizen asked De Cock to baptize his child. The child in question was already three years old but had not yet been baptized. When De Cock asked Schoonoort why he had not asked his own pastor, Meijer-Brouwer, to administer the sacrament, Schoonoort answered that he could not in good conscience answer yes to one of the questions asked in the Form for Baptism, to wit: "Do you believe that the true doctrines of the Old and New Testament are preached in this church?" He believed, he said, that these doctrines were not preached in his church; therefore, he had not presented his child for baptism.[1]

Since Schoonoort belonged to the Uithuizen Reformed Church, De Cock relayed this information to Vander Werp. The two discussed the matter, knowing that there were many more parents who felt they could not in good conscience have their children baptized by pastors whom they believed were not teaching the true doctrines of the church. Both men also realized that if De Cock would baptize this child, whose parents were not members of his congregation, he would stir up serious trouble. He took several months to weigh the matter and to seek advice from others.[2] There was, however, no church law against a minister

[1] J. C. van der Does, *De Afscheiding in haar wording en beginperiode* 2nd ed. (Delft: Naamlooze Vennootschap W.D. Meinema, 1934), 56-58.
[2] He wrote letters asking for advice to the Rev. Molenaar of The Hague, and to Baron Cornelis van Zuylen van Nijevelt (1777-1833). Molenaar suggested he proceed very

Middelstum Classis meeting room

baptizing a child not belonging to his congregation. When De Cock approached his consistory about the matter, it recommended that God be obeyed rather than man, regardless of the consequences, and encouraged De Cock to baptize the child. On Sunday, September 29, 1833, De Cock baptized the Schoonoort child. Once the child's name was entered into the baptismal register of the Ulrum Reformed Church and the deed done, De Cock baptized sixteen more children from various congregations in the surrounding area.[3]

In November 1833, De Cock published his answer to Meijer-Brouwer and Benthem-Reddingius in a booklet titled, *Defense of the True Reformed Doctrine and of the True Reformed Believers. Attacked and Exposed by Two So-called Reformed Pastors, or the Sheepfold of Christ Attacked by Two Wolves and Defended by H. De Cock, Reformed Pastor at Ulrum.*[4] The title was anything but friendly and the term "wolves" was not especially tactful.

carefully. Because Baron van Zuylen, a member of the Réveil in the Netherlands, passed away in May he could not answer De Cock. Baron van Zuylen's pamphlet, *Onze Redding* [*Our Salvation*], helped De Cock understand the relationship between doctrine and practice, and De Cock valued his advice.

[3] J. A. Wormser, *Een schat in aarden vaten, Eerste Serie III,* "*Werken zoolang het dag is.*" *Het leven van Hendrik De Cock* (Nijverdal: Bosch, 1915), 41. Included in the children baptized by De Cock on November 17, 1833 was one child of Luitsen Dijkstra (leader of the Seceders in Smilde), born June 14, 1832.

[4] H. De Cock, *Verdediging van de ware Gereformeerde leer en van de ware Gereformeerden bestreden door twee zoogenaamde Gereformeerde leeraars, of: De schaapskooi van Christus aangetast door twee wolven en verdedigd* (Groningen: Bolt, 1833).

Middelstum: Building where disciplinary meeting
was held December 19, 1833

For baptizing children from other congregations and for publishing this pamphlet, which made harsh judgments against his fellow pastors, De Cock had a formal complaint brought against him by a member of one of the churches in his classis.[5] On November 18, 1833, a committee of the classis came to the parsonage in Ulrum and asked him pointblank whether he had baptized children belonging to other congregations and whether he intended to continue doing so. [6] To both questions De Cock answered, "Yes, unless there is a church order rule that forbids me to do so." On December 18, a second complaint was lodged, and he was asked to appear before a committee of the classis in Middelstum. At that meeting he was asked if he was teaching the catechism to members of other congregations and if he was the writer of the brochure against Brouwer and Reddingius, and if so, was he prepared to recant the statements made therein? De Cock said he could not do so, and since he was not allowed to defend himself, the meeting adjourned.

On Friday, December 20, 1833, the committee sent De Cock its verdict: "H. De Cock will be suspended from his position as pastor for the time being without loss of salary." De Cock's congregation came to his defense immediately by sending a letter to the committee of the

[5]   Classis Middelstum.
[6]   Consisting of A. Rutgers, H. Warmolts, and P. Rutgers.

classis asking it to provide proof of a church rule forbidding De Cock to baptize children from other congregations. The letter also stated that it was unjust to punish De Cock for writing against Brouwer and Reddingius, while the latter had not been punished for writing against De Cock.

The next day, Saturday, Vander Werp, along with some of De Cock's followers, met in the home of the widow Geesje Koster, to deliberate their next move.[7] They had to decide who should preach on Sunday, and for the two services on Christmas Day. The classis had scheduled A. Du Cloux, the pastor from Vierhuizen to lead the Sunday service. However, the Ulrum congregation, upset by this action, believed that De Cock should preach. Several members told De Cock that he could count on a large following willing to use force, if necessary. But De Cock, citing scripture, cautioned against this. He believed he should obey the ecclesiastical authorities and refrain from leading the worship service.[8]

That Sunday, as the church bells called the faithful to worship, Vander Werp watched from the parsonage window to see if anyone would attend services. A few people had already entered the church when he saw Du Cloux, apparently fearing trouble, march into town with a sizable group of armed militia. While the militia stationed themselves around the outside of the church, Du Cloux entered without resistance.[9] Most members of the congregation had stayed home; others met with De Cock in the home of the widow Koster. Here, again, De Cock refused to preach, saying it would be a breach of the conditions imposed upon him. Instead, he asked Dijkstra, the peat farmer from Smilde who happened to be present, to lead those assembled in worship and speak a few uplifting words.[10] Although De Cock's indictment had

[7]   Wesseling, *Groningerland,* 1: 46-47. Geesje Harms Hulshoff, widow of Freerk Tjipkes Koster, owned a wagon making and cooper business on Noorderstraat and Schapenweg. Her home was used as the meeting place for the Seceders at great cost to her as she was fined several times.
[8]   F. L. Bos, *Kruisdominees: Figuren uit de Gereformeerde Kerk onder 't Kruis* (Kampen: Kok, 1953), 133.
[9]   A.P.A. du Cloux was a twenty-six-year-old pastor who had been pastor in Vierhuizen for only two years when the *Afscheiding* took place. At first he was very opposed to the movement, but later his stance softened.
[10] S. J. Th. Homan, "Cocksianen in Drenthe," *Nieuwe Drentse Volksalmanak* (1984): 3-17. Luitsen Jochems Dijkstra, born at Gorredijk, Friesland on July 31, 1798, was a sheepherder. He married Grietje Alberts Eendvogel, on January 5, 1801, at Smilde, and became a peat farmer. In 1842 he was ordained to the ministry and served as pastor at Steenwijk until his death in 1871.

Koster house and cooper shop

been against preaching, it had not been against prayer. He therefore couched his sermon within the prayer lasting nearly an hour. Lay ministers, who were not permitted to preach without proper license, often used this tactic very effectively as well. After all, one could hardly prevent someone from praying![11]

That De Cock had chosen the unschooled peat farmer to lead the gathering did not surprise Vander Werp. Dijkstra had been exhorting as a lay preacher in Smilde for some time and therefore had experience. Perhaps it was at these meetings that Vander Werp began to foster a desire also to exhort. He had a fine reading and singing voice and had been front and center in all the goings-on. Knowing he could do it, he decided to ask De Cock to let him lead sometime.

About this time another booklet was being circulated, generally thought to have been written by Hofstede de Groot. De Groot, a professor of theology at the University of Groningen, exercised considerable influence in theological matters in the northern provinces. When he failed to restrain De Cock by letter, De Groot published a small booklet entitled, *Wien zult gij gelooven, den mensch of God?* or *Whom will you believe, God or man?*[12] By *man*, de Groot meant De Cock's emphasis on

[11] H. J. Brinks, "Germans in the Christian Reformed Church 1857-1872," *Origins*, 9/2 (1991): 40.
[12] P. Hofstede de Groot, *Wien zult gij gelooven, den mensch of God?* (Published anonymously, 1833).

VERDEDIGING

VAN DE

WARE GEREFORMEERDE LEER

EN VAN DE

WARE GEREFORMEERDEN,

bestreden en ten toon gesteld

DOOR TWEE ZOOGENAAMDE

GEREFORMEERDE LEERAARS,

OF DE

SCHAAPSKOOI VAN CHRISTUS

aangetast door TWEE WOLVEN en verdedigd

DOOR

H. DE COCK,

GEREFORMEERD LEERAAR TE *ULRUM.*

PHILIPP. 3 : 2. Ziet op de honden, ziet op de kwade arbeiders, ziet op de versnijding.

JOHANNES. Geliefden gelooft niet eenen iegelijken geest, maar beproeft de geesten, of zij uit God zijn : want vele valsche profeten zijn uitgegaan in de wereld.

2 COR. 4 : 3, 4, 5. Indien ook ons Evangelium bedekt is, zoo is het bedekt in de gene die verloren gaan, in dewelke de God dezer eeuwe de zinnen verblind heeft, enz.

TE GRONINGEN, BIJ
J. H. BOLT, 1833.

Cover of *Verdediging*

John Calvin's theology, rather than on Jesus' law of love. The booklet's twelve pages are divided into two columns with the headings, "Man's Word" and "God's Word," and rejects the doctrine of divine election.

De Cock, too busy himself as he admits in the preface, or perhaps because his publication against Meijer-Brouwer and Reddingius had caused him so much trouble already, asked Vander Werp and Dijkstra to write a rebuttal. Pleased to be given such an important task in the struggle against liberalism, these two unlettered men wrote *Public Protest*.[13] This booklet, too, would have grave repercussions, and no wonder. In the first thirty-two pages, Vander Werp refutes De Groot's statements point by point, citing numerous texts and using the same harsh language as his mentor. Even as De Cock referred to the two Reformed pastors as "wolves in sheep's clothing" in his booklet, Vander Werp accuses the Reformed pastors of turning the Reformed church into a pigsty.[14] The second half of the booklet consists of 115 four-line verses of poetry written by Luitsen Dijkstra. These last twenty pages, which read more easily and have a less strident tone, could be bought separately for 7 ½ cents; the total booklet sold for 12 ½ cents.

De Groot believed that De Cock had humiliated him by allowing two young men without proper theological training to contest him as equals in a theological debate. De Cock's thinking, on the other hand, was that an unlettered and unlearned person endowed with the Holy Spirit was an equal match for a learned one.[15] Nevertheless, the effects of De Groot's wrath were soon felt. Irritated at being bested by a third-rank teacher's assistant, De Groot as school supervisor for the province of Groningen, instructed Pietersen to dismiss Vander Werp. Disregarding Pietersen's petitions as well as those of the children's parents, De Groot prevailed; in May 1834 Vander Werp was ousted as teacher not only from Houwerzijl, but also from the entire province. Grounds for dismissal were that De Groot did not want *onzuivere godsdienst*, or unsound religion, to be taught in the schools in his

---

[13] H. De Cock, *Openlijk protest en dichtregelen tegen zeker blauwboekje, getiteld: "Wien moet men gelooven den mensch of God?"* (Veendam: Mulder, 1834). De Cock's name is on the cover, but on the inside cover he credits Vander Werp and Dijkstra with the writing. In fact, in his preface, De Cock states that he had asked these two ordinary men, considered "dumb and uneducated" by worldly standards, to show that they could be used to shame the wise of this world. The complete text of this booklet is found in Hendrik De Cock, *Verzamelde Geschriften*, 2 vols. (Houten: Den Hertog, 1984), 1: 115-47.

[14] Ibid., 4, "Om maar een zwijnenkot van Neerlands Kerk te maken."

[15] Wesseling, *Groningerland*, 2:107.

Petrus Hofstede
de Groot

district. So six months before the official *Afscheiding* took place, Vander Werp already felt the sting of religious nonconformity.

Years later, at the request of De Cock's son, Helenius, Vander Werp wrote about this experience.

> When Mr. Van Kleeff was school supervisor here, I was allowed to teach without hindrance. But as soon as Hofstede de Groot became supervisor, Wieko Pietersen received instructions to dismiss me. Actions taken on my behalf by Mr. Pietersen, and by the congregation proved futile. Another teacher was from Groningen, and I had to leave. A reason for my dismissal was never given, even though I tried very hard to find out why. In the three years that I taught I never had a municipal official or a district supervisor observe my teaching. Neither was I ever called to give an account of my teaching. I do know that the minister of the parish did not agree with our religious viewpoint, but how would he know since he never came to classroom, nor sent his children to our school? They were hostile to me because of the influence I had speaking the truth to many of the elderly, who attended your father's church and because I taught the children

lessons based on biblical principles. De Groot thought he had to guard against "unsound" doctrine being taught, calling the doctrine of true saving grace "unsound." [16]

But even though he spoke of being silent when persecuted for his faith in his July 30, 1832, letter to his parents, Vander Werp responded to his dismissal by writing a long letter to King William I. In it he bewailed the injustice done to him: that he was dismissed without a hearing, without a visit to his classroom from either the district or provincial authorities, and without being given any reason for his dismissal. In his appeal, he reminded the king of his duty as ruler to be fair and just, and urged the king to adjudicate his case.[17] It is not known whether the king, who was very much in favor of the public school system, ever answered young Vander Werp.

Vander Werp's abrupt dismissal from his teaching position presented a real predicament for him—where should he go now, and how could he make a living? Going back to his parents in Uithuizen was out of the question. Economically they were in no position to help him. They had three more children: Wobbenius, born in 1824; Grietje, born in 1827; and Willem, born in 1829. In fact, by 1828 father Johannes had to augment his income by taking on additional work as assistant to the custodian of his church. According to Ulrum's mayor, the followers of De Cock were creating bitter enmity in the town's families, pitting husband against wife and children against their parents.[18] The elder Vander Werps' continued support of their pastor, Meijer-Brouwer, may also have created a division between them and their son. Adherents of De Cock had destroyed Uithuizen's peace, and there was no denying that their son had become one of De Cock's strongest adherents.

As long as Hofstede De Groot continued as school supervisor for Groningen, Vander Werp would not be able to teach in the province. Neither had he been trained for any other kind of work. When he explained his problem to De Cock, the latter took him into his home to

---

[16] G. Keizer, "Documenten bezwarend voor het karakter van Professor Hofstede de Groot," *Gereformeerd Theologish Tijdschrift*, Vol. 21, No. 9 (January 1921): 321. "Men was mij vijandig om de invloed, die ik door de waarheid op vele bejaarde mensen uitoefende, die deswege bij uw vader ter kerk gingen en omdat ik de kinderen op bijbelse gronden onderwees. Hofstede de Groot meende er voor te moeten zorgen dat er geen onzuivere godsdienstgronden in de school onderwezen werden, noemende de ware zaligmakende vrije-genadeleer een onzuivere godsdienstleer."

[17] Ibid, 323-29.

[18] Wesseling, *Groningerland*, 2: 47.

assist him full time with his enormous amount of paper work. De Cock, feeling he was somewhat to blame for Vander Werp's dismissal, wrote on his behalf to P. J. Baron van Zuylen van Nijevelt, who wrote back in a letter dated July 29, 1834, "Brother Vander Werp's dismissal saddens me; however, I am at present not able to help him, but will not forget him."[19]

Whether Vander Werp suggested it to De Cock or De Cock to Vander Werp is not known, but by June Vander Werp was also helping out in the gatherings at the widow Koster's by reading sermons. On Friday, June 8, in the company of some fifty people, he read a sermon by Herman F. Kohlbrügge, a Dutch-German theologian. Before long he put away the prepared sermons and spoke from his own heart wherever and whenever he could.

Although De Cock had been suspended from preaching, he was allowed the use of the parsonage, which through autumn 1834 became a hub of activity. The weather that summer remained fair and dry, so that almost daily delegations from all over the northern provinces trekked to the Ulrum parsonage to discuss their church situations. Besides the visits, many letters arrived daily, which also needed to be answered. While De Cock dictated, Vander Werp wrote. A second, handwritten copy was made of each piece of correspondence that went out.

Even without the many strangers coming into Ulrum, tensions were running high in the town. The mayor of Ulrum considered De Cock's teachings dangerous. He accused De Cock of stirring up hatred against people who did not agree with him and had even heard De Cock say "that he hoped those false teachers, meaning those Reformed Church pastors, might be destroyed, that an earthquake would open up the earth and swallow them up alive."[20] Vander Werp was learning the language of spiritual warfare from his mentor—language he would use himself time and again.

Early in the spring of 1834, De Cock ceased all his pastoral duties in order to focus on getting his suspension reversed. He decided to plead his case before a higher body, the Provincial Synodical Committee, and if that failed he would go to the king, who at one time had approved his appointment as a minister of the gospel. On March 11, 1834, he was called to appear in Groningen to defend himself. This body reacted

---

[19] Keizer, *Afscheiding*, 419. Baron Paulus Jacob van Zuylen van Nijevelt (1775-1855) was a brother to Cornelis Baron van Zuylen van Nijeveldt. See note 2.

[20] Wesseling, *Groningerland*, 1: 47.

even more unfavorably against him. Whereas his classis suspension had been for an indefinite period and with pay, this committee gave him a two-year suspension with loss of salary. This heavy punishment was given not so much for baptizing or catechizing children of other congregations—those charges were dropped—but for the complaint about the brochure against Meijer-Brouwer and Reddingius. On behalf of the consistory of Ulrum, De Cock and two members decided to take their case directly to King William I. During their three-week trip south, they visited several people sympathetic to their cause, including Hendrik P. Scholte in Doeveren, a friend of De Cock, before arriving in The Hague.[21] Their audience with the king on May 14 held little hope; the king, it seemed, had no tolerance for Seceders. As far as he was concerned, people opposing the state of affairs in the Reformed Church were "schismatic, fomentors of unrest, and secret agitators."[22]

While the Dutch constitution allowed for freedom of religion, there was a subtle catch in the wording. It granted freedom to all *existing* religions, not freedom to form *new* ones. De Cock's argument that all he really wanted was to practice the historic religion as outlined by the Synod of Dort found no favor with a king who personally had rewritten the rules of the Reformed Church in 1816.

Back home in Ulrum, as the spring of 1834 turned to summer and the summer to fall, De Cock wrote pamphlet after pamphlet defending his position. Most of these were printed at his own expense by T. E. Mulder, a secessionist sympathizer, in Veendam. Earlier in 1833, De Cock had Mulder reprint the Church Order of Dordt, and no doubt Vander Werp studied this document from cover to cover. Over the weeks and months his knowledge of doctrine, confessional statements, and church order crystallized.

[21] H. De Cock, *Hendrik De Cock, Eerste Afgescheiden Predikant in Nederland* (Delfzijl, Jan Haan, 1886), 97. Hendrik Scholte and De Cock first became acquainted when Scholte wrote to De Cock December 6, 1833, stating that he had purchased and read two of De Cock's pamphlets. The two began a correspondence which led to a friendship. H. Bouwman, *Crisis der Jeugd* (Kampen: Kok, 1914), 45. Seven years later, after the Synod of 1840 deposed Scholte, De Cock and Scholte no longer had any contact.

[22] Robert P. Swierenga and Elton J. Bruins, *Family Quarrels in the Dutch Reformed Churches in the Nineteenth Century,* The Pillar Church Sesquicentennial Lectures (Grand Rapids: Eerdmans, 1999), 23. See also G. P. Marang, *De Zwijndrechtsche Nieuwlichters* (Dordrecht: De Graaf, 1909), 110-14. King William I apparently had been lenient towards a small group of dissenters from the Reformed Church who had taken advantage of this leniency, and he classed this new group known as Seceders in the same category as the *Nieuwlichters.*

Perhaps due to the popularity of Dijkstra's rhymed version of the *Public Protest*, which he and Vander Werp had written earlier, the two collaborated in writing a rhymed treatise on two topics: *Descriptions of the Beasts from the Pit*, based on Revelation 9 (sixty-six four-line verses), and *The Old Hebrew Language regarding Circumcision of the Heart or The Hebrew Word Shibboleth*, based on Romans 2: 28, 29, Judges 12:16, and Nehemiah 13:23-25 (78 four-line verses). On the cover, the two refer to themselves as "friends of the truth," and below his name on the cover Vander Werp wrote, "D. van der Werp, who for the sake of the truth was dismissed as schoolteacher of Houwerzijl, and currently a member of the living Reformed Church at Ulrum."

In both poems, De Cock is portrayed as the hero battling the beast bent on destroying the church. A sample of verses indicates that any lingering allegiance Vander Werp may have held to his parents' faith and church had by now shifted irrevocably to De Cock's vision of the church.

> De Cock esteemed sir,
> No matter how the mockers tremble
> We desire all the more,
> To be upheld by you. (verse 36)
> If you are being hated
> Enduring much disrespect.
> Remember that you are standing
> On Zion's firm walls. (verse 37)
> Stand firm, esteemed hero.
> Remember, no matter how those modernists rave,
> Do not fear their bluster
> Regard them to be but fools. (verse 39)

T. E. Mulder, De Cock's publisher at Veendam, also published Vander Werp's booklet in 1834. Because there is no price printed on the cover, it may be that Vander Werp had it printed at his own expense and distributed it himself. Distribution of pamphlets was readily accomplished by *beurtschippers* along the nation's waterways, and by backpacking peddlers along inland roads. De Cock's books, on the whole, were sold in bookstores and by colporteurs. By the end of the summer, the larger part of the population had formed an opinion and was choosing sides; the battle lines between De Cock's adherents and his opponents were drawn so taut, they would soon snap.

CHAPTER 5

Secession

Sunday evening, October 19, 1834, a visibly shaken Vander Werp arrived at his brother's boat moored in Zoutkamp. Because Christian schippers did not sail on Sundays, Vander Werp knew exactly where to find Jan Hendrik. They had remained close ever since their childhood on their parents' boat and their school days in Uithuizen. Jan Hendrik had followed in his father's former profession of beurtschipper, but he had followed in his brother's spiritual footsteps. And because Jan Hendrik was also deeply involved with those who favored seceding from the Reformed Church, Vander Werp knew he was safe with his brother. Only after Jan Hendrik had calmed Vander Werp with food and a fresh pipe of tobacco did he hear the whole story of the events of the past couple of weeks that would have such far-reaching consequences in their lives. How had it come about?

Vander Werp described De Cock's dilemma. Should he try to persuade the Provincial Board of his regret about the baptisms and the booklets and ask to be reinstated as pastor? And what form should this regret take? He also weighed the idea of officially seceding from the Reformed Church. There were many who urged him to do so, but he hesitated to break up the body of Christ. On July 31, 1834, he wrote to the Provincial Board asking on what conditions he could be reinstated. The board was in the same quandary. It did not want a secession on its hands, but at the same time it wanted to smooth the ruffled feathers of Meijer-Brouwer and Reddingius. The board admonished De Cock

Hendrik Scholte

not to write any more pamphlets with inflammatory remarks, and it demanded a full retraction of the statements in his brochures. Early in October De Cock met with the board, but it turned out to be another futile meeting. As much as he wanted peace, he could not deny his beliefs. Without gaining any ground on either side, other than that De Cock promised to keep strictly to church rules, the meeting was adjourned.

When De Cock arrived back in Ulrum, Hendrik Scholte, his friend from Doeveren, was waiting for him. Scholte had traveled to the northern province to visit a sick relative, and while there had heard about his friend's impasse and decided to come to his support. That evening, Thursday, October 9, Scholte preached to an overflow crowd in Geesje Koster's cooper shop. He promised to preach again that Sunday in church; however, he first had to seek permission from the church counselor. When he asked, he was denied permission. Instead, the counselor led the service himself. From far and near, hundreds of

Ulrum: Interior of Dutch Reformed Church

people had come by boat, by wagon, and on foot hoping to hear Scholte preach. Packed into the full church, the people listened quietly during the counselor's preaching, but after the service, when De Cock stood up and asked if Scholte could preach in the afternoon, that request was also denied. The congregation, upset by this turn of events, streamed forward to the pulpit and would have thrown out the counselor had not Scholte intervened.

Now that Scholte had gained firsthand knowledge of the situation, he urged De Cock to consider seceding, and that weekend Scholte and De Cock discussed the idea of seceding from the established church. However, Helenius De Cock, Hendrik De Cock's son, states, "During Rev. Scholte's stay, no decision to secede was made. At his departure he himself did not know but that father would seek another audience with the king and the synodical committee."[1] No doubt Vander Werp listened in on the debate whenever he could. Scholte left on Monday without the two having come to any decision. But by Tuesday, October 14, De Cock saw no alternative but to secede.

---

[1]   De Cock. *Hendrik De Cock,* 297. "Tijdens het verblijf van Ds. Scholte werd er echter niet tot de afscheiding besloten. Bij zijn vertrek wist hij zelfs nog niet anders, dan dat vader zich nog tot den koning en de synodale commissie wenden wilde."

Soldiers sent to Ulrum
to keep the peace

That evening the congregation gathered, except for a few members who did not wish to secede, and, with De Cock as its pastor, formally separated itself from the Reformed Church. The following Sunday the people marched en masse to the church building, mistakenly thinking it was theirs. The police had been informed and would not allow De Cock access to the pulpit. When Johannes van der Helm from Niekerk, who had been called to preach that day, attempted to gain access to the pulpit, the people would not let him pass.[2] Fearing trouble, he left. De Cock then tried to make his way to the stairs of the pulpit but was halted by an officer. Still determined to preach, he climbed on one of the front pews and preached from there. After the service, when the

---

[2]   J. P. van der Helm (1778-1857).

Ulrum parsonage

people had left the church, the doors were locked behind them. Since they were now effectively barred from their building, they held their afternoon service outside. The Secession had become fact; there was no going back.

Tensions ran high during the week that followed, and the authorities, fearing another mob the following Sunday, called in the military. On the Saturday preceding, one hundred soldiers marched into Ulrum, took over the town, and posted twelve men in the parsonage. No one was allowed in or out of the house. Vander Werp, working on some correspondence, was asked if he was a member of the family. When he said no, they pushed him out the door and told him to get out of town.[3]

With nowhere else to go, Vander Werp made his way to Zoutkamp to Jan Hendrik's boat. At least he was free. The court in Appingedam accused De Cock of creating civil unrest, fined him 150 guilders, and sentenced him to three months in jail. He was to begin serving his sentence November 28. Even before his release, De Cock's wife was told to vacate the parsonage, and she began to look for a place to live.[4]

Discussing his limited options with Jan Hendrik, Vander Werp decided that perhaps he should accept Dijkstra's invitation to come to Smilde. Dijkstra hoped that as soon as the people in Smilde had formed

[3]   Van der Does, *De Afscheiding*, 71.
[4]   De Cock, *Hendrik De Cock*, 372.

a Secession congregation, they would also start a Christian school for their children. Some time previous he had asked Vander Werp to move there and be their teacher. Since Vander Werp had no other options, he decided to head for Smilde in the morning.

CHAPTER 6

Teaching and Preaching in Smilde

Jan Hendrik ferried his brother as far as Grijpskerk. From there Vander Werp continued his journey by foot and canal boat, arriving in Smilde the first day of November. There, he soon found himself the center of attention, as the secession-minded Christians in the community were eager to hear about the events in Ulrum. For the next several days, Vander Werp, who boarded with the Sickens family, met with various families in the area to discuss secession matters.

Sunday, November 9, 1834, at Dijkstra's invitation, Vander Werp led a large group in worship, after which the former read the procedures for secession. The group decided to meet the following Friday to sign the Act of Secession. They dispatched Dijkstra to Ulrum to bring De Cock to Smilde to formally organize the congregation.[1] When De Cock arrived, he brought with him the news that Scholte had also seceded with his congregation from the Reformed Church in Doeveren—news that greatly encouraged the Ulrum and Smilde seceders.[2]

The first order of business for the leaders in Smilde was the logistics of meeting in groups of less than twenty. In order to prevent people from meeting in large groups and causing civil unrest, the

---

[1] Only ordained ministers had the authority to install elders and deacons, and so form a legitimate congregation.

[2] For all data regarding the Secession at Smilde see Homan, "Cocksianen in Drenthe," 3-17. Also see De Rover-Wijnstekers, Elly, *De Afscheiding van 1823 te Smilde*, Een eindscriptie van de HBO-Theologie te Windesheim, May 2000, published at http://members.tripod.lycos.nl/veldeling/smilde.htm.

government had dusted off an old law still on the books from the years of French annexation that made it unlawful to meet in groups of twenty or more. The Seceders decided to abide by the law and organized themselves into six cells of believers. At first Sickens and Vander Werp were against this arrangement, preferring to defy the rule, but caution prevailed, and Dijkstra, Sickens, and Vander Werp were each assigned to take turns leading the groups in worship as lay preachers. Only twenty-three, Vander Werp spoke fervently and emotionally to these groups about the need to establish a true church, which was faithful to the Word of God as reflected in the Canons of Dort, the Heidelberg Catechism, and the Belgic Confession. His words touched their hearts as well as their minds. As he was asked again and again to lead services, his gift for preaching became more and more evident.

Another item heavy on the hearts of the *Afgescheiden* at Smilde and elsewhere concerned the school situation. Many parents were keeping their children out of school because of new state requirements barring the Bible and the Heidelberg Catechism from being taught in the public schools, and also because in 1823 the state had decreed that all children attending school be immunized against smallpox.[3]

Many of the Seceders were against vaccination. They reasoned that Jesus clearly stated, "It is not the healthy who need a doctor."[4] Also, the Heidelberg Catechism in Lord's Day 10 states that "health and sickness come to us not by chance but from his fatherly hand." So anyone using vaccination was running ahead of the Lord by protecting himself against any chastisement the Lord might want to impose upon him. Nevertheless, unless a child came to school with proof of vaccination, he or she was not allowed to attend.

Dijkstra and two other men formed a Christian school board and hired Vander Werp to teach at five cents per child per week. The day after they had pledged to incorporate themselves as an *Afgescheiden* congregation, they brought their children to the barn of Willem Snippe to begin school. Taking in his new teaching surroundings, Vander Werp undoubtedly was reminded of Jesus' humble beginnings in a barn. Tables and benches had been set up for the pupils in one corner of Snippe's barn, while in another corner there were pens for pigs,

---

[3]   For a study on the school situation at the time, see J. Sheeres, "The Struggle for the Souls of the Children: The Effects of the Dutch Education Law of 1806 on the Emigration of 1847," *The Dutch in Urban America* (Holland, Mich: Association for the Advancement of Dutch American Studies, 2004), 34-47.

[4]   Matthew 9:12, NIV.

cattle, and poultry. Faggots of dried heather for fuel and hay for the cattle were stored in yet another corner. Twenty children attended the first day. This became the very first organized private school based on Reformed teachings in the Netherlands, with Vander Werp as the first teacher. The date was November 10, 1834.

In their enthusiasm, or perhaps their ignorance, the organizers made a grave error by not applying for permission from the provincial authorities to operate a private school. They also neglected to note that H. Doorenbos, pastor of the Smilde Reformed Church and school supervisor for the district, had kept them under strict surveillance. Doorenbos's preaching had not sat well with the conservative element of Smilde's Reformed Church. Soon after his arrival in 1820, the congregants quietly began to stay away from the services, meeting instead in conventicles led by lay preachers. Now seeing how this new school was draining students from the existing state-run public school, Doorenbos wrote immediately to the governor of the province of Drenthe, citing names and places and calling Vander Werp a troublemaker who defied the existing school laws. The letter, dated November 11, 1834, brought swift retribution.

On November 13, at eleven in the morning, the mayor, a policeman, and a municipal clerk appeared in the barn with a court order to fine Vander Werp for operating a public school without proper permission.[5] They also declared the schoolroom a fire hazard and an unhealthy place. They closed it the same day. According to Mayor Kymmell, "The children were so afraid of that dark place and the fiery teacher that some had run away crying, while others could not sleep at night."[6]

Vander Werp decided not to challenge the law. He gave up his teaching career, but not without consequences. For teaching without a license he was fined fifty guilders and court costs of two guilders and thirty-nine cents—a hefty sum for someone getting paid only in nickels.[7]

---

[5]   See appendix 2 for the text of this interrogation.

[6]   Mayor Kymmell to Provincial Governor, dated November 24, 1834. Verzonden Brieven [Sent Letters] 1834-1836. Gemeente Archief, Smilde, the Netherlands.

[7]   Wesseling, *Groningerland*, 2: 262. The congregation of Wildervank gathered twelve guilders toward Vander Werp's fine and court costs in Assen for teaching without a permit. Perhaps there were others who helped as well, because without paying the debt, he would have had to serve jail time, and there is no record of him going to jail.

Barred from teaching in the provinces of Groningen and Drenthe, Douwe turned to his other love—preaching. Using Smilde as his headquarters, he traveled the countryside conducting services and teaching catechism at newly formed *Afgescheiden* congregations. When the occasion presented itself, he would also teach reading and writing in his catechism classes so his students could read their catechism lessons on their own.

Two days before Christmas, Hendrik Sickens and Vander Werp traveled to Groningen to visit De Cock, who had begun serving his three-month jail sentence November 28, 1834. Rather than being incarcerated in a maximum-security style prison, De Cock was housed in the *Correctie* or *Spinhuis* on Zoutstraat in Groningen, where, because he paid for it himself, he was allowed a private room, stove, and bed. He also paid for his own food. Many of those who visited him brought along food for him, and Sickens, being the prosperous farmer he was, probably also came bearing gifts. De Cock was allowed three visitors per day, one at a time, under supervision of the prison guard. Although their discussion was monitored, there is no doubt that De Cock encouraged Vander Werp to keep on preaching and teaching in his absence.[8]

Indeed, Vander Werp had found his calling in preaching the Word. In March of that year, a Secessionist congregation was organized in Dwingelo, and called him as its regular lay pastor. While there, it is said that he preached such fiery messages that many of the women in the audience fainted. These pious people were so gripped in their hearts by their sinful state that they would pass out.[9] The authorities, however, were not pleased with such behavior. The mayor reported to the provincial governor, "For several months he [Vander Werp] has

[8]   Ibid, 1: 222-31. According to Wesseling, the first visitor December 23, was H. Sickens, and the second was a van der Werf, but he guessed at who this might be and added an additional "f" to make it van der Werff. See H. Veldman, *Hendrik de Cock – Afgescheiden en toch betrokken!* (Bedum, Cedrus, 2004). Dr. Veldman has recently reexamined the life of Hendrik De Cock and claims that De Cock was a sloppy writer who often misspelled names and he is certain that *van der Werf* should be *van der Werp*, that it was Vander Werp who visited De Cock right after Sickens on December 23. The original diary rests in the Municipal Archives in Kampen, the Netherlands (Archief De Cock, nrs. I,1,3). Also see Keizer, *Afscheiding van 1834*, p. 40 regarding De Cock's very sloppy penmanship leading to many errors in his publications.

[9]   J. Kok, *Meister Albert en zijn zonen: Uit de geschiedenis der Afscheiding in Drenthe* (Kampen: Kok 1909), 189.

Jail in Groningen where De Cock was incarcerated

been roaming around here exhorting where he can, and his removal is very much desired." [10]

However, Vander Werp was not the only one who could be accused of stirring up the people to the point of fainting. During those turbulent years many lay preachers and self-appointed prophets roamed through the provinces, so that the authorities were wary and weary of all of them, including Vander Werp. [11]

After his release from jail in February 1835, De Cock also moved to Smilde. Hendrik Sickens invited the entire De Cock family to move in with his family. From this location, De Cock and Vander Werp made

---

[10] De Rover-Wijnstekers, *De Afscheiding van 1823 te Smilde*, unpaginated. "Sedert maanden hier reeds rond gezworven hebbende en waar hij kan oefening houdende wordt zijne verwijdering zeer gewenscht."

[11] Kok, *Meister Albert*, 76-9. Jan de Blauw, a baker from St. Johannesga in Friesland, also called *Vrome* Jan [Pious John], traveled with a woman [not his wife] by the name of Jakobje, who according to *Vrome* Jan, was a prophetess and filled with the Spirit. They would travel through Friesland, Drenthe, and Groningen bringing confusion wherever they went. Jan announced that he had been "called" to preach the imminent return of Jesus, and for people to prepare themselves. Horrible things would happen and that in Dwingelo blood would flow. Jacobje filled with the "spirit" would begin to prophesy, and because she was able to give her words a veneer of piety, many took this for the truth. Mass hysteria followed these events. Gold and silver jewelry was cast aside, paintings and mirrors were destroyed, and pages containing hymns were cut out of the hymnal and burned along with worldly

visits to conventicles in the area that were interested in joining the Secession. Thursday, March 12, 1835, De Cock, his wife, and Vander Werp traveled by canal boat to Kampen to attend just such a meeting in the home of Lammert Ensing on the Rademarkt. Derk Hoksbergen, one of those present, told the others how he had met De Cock. Hoksbergen and a friend, Frans Gunning, had heard a lot about De Cock, but had never met him or heard him preach. One day the two had to be in Groningen to sell some horses, and while there they heard that De Cock was in the city and that he would preach. They hurried to the place and stayed not only for the preaching, but also for the organization of a new congregation. In short, they were so encouraged and engrossed by all that was happening that they totally forgot their original mission to Groningen.[12]

Vander Werp had heard similar stories. How the beekeepers from Drenthe, on their annual trek north to the province of Groningen to put their hives in the rapeseed fields there, would stop over on Sunday to hear De Cock preach and then bring the message back to their hometowns. It never ceased to amaze him how God used ordinary means to bring his chosen ones to a saving knowledge of the gospel.

He himself hoped to be ordained, not only to proclaim the gospel, but to administer the sacraments as well. With many congregations being formed and only two ordained pastors, there was a severe shortage of ordained ministers, and it made sense to ordain those gifted for office. The church order had made provisions for such an ordination in times of great need. The first prerequisite had been met when Dwingelo called Vander Werp to be its regular lay pastor, and no doubt the matter was discussed. De Cock decided to write to Scholte, who had served him with advice before; however, Scholte, in a letter dated March 3, 1835, wrote back,

> books. With great ceremony Jan would make bonfires to destroy the banned materials. He ordered the people to paint their houses black and live communally sharing everything. On one journey he was able to draw people from Wapse, Wapserveen, and Diever and altogether in four wagons descended on Dwingelo, overwhelming the pious people there. In Dwingelo, while trying to convince a wealthy widow to take off her golden headpiece and hand over her psalter to have the offending pages cut out, she challenged him, and then Jacobje began to scream a series of "woes to the wealthy."

12   Wesseling, *Groningerland*, 2: 132. On June 3, 1835, the *Afgescheiden* Church in Kampen was organized; De Cock installed Derk Hoksbergen (1800-1870) as elder. Hoksbergen would later join the *Kruisgezinden*, and not happy with them either formed his own church in 1838, the Dordts Gereformeerden van Hoksbergen.

As far as ordaining Vander Werp to ministerial status, I cannot at this time, condone it; he can preach the Word, in season and out, but you yourself can administer the sacrament of baptism as an ordained pastor; about this matter, I am considering the words of the Apostles, "do not lay hands on anyone in haste."[13]

Understandably, Vander Werp was disappointed in the outcome. He stayed in the area for another couple of months, but in May, when De Cock was appointed pastor for the surrounding Secessionist churches within a seventy-five kilometer radius of Smilde, he advised Vander Werp to return to Groningen to teach and preach in that province.

[13]   Keizer, *Afscheiding*, 94. "Wat het beroepen van Van der Werp als leeraar betreft, ook dit kan ik tot nog toe niet goedkeuren, het woord spreken en aanhouden tijdig en ontijdig, dit kan hij nu ook doen, het Sacrament des doops bedienen, dit kunt gij doen als geordend leeraar; ik dacht bij dit stuk aan de Apostolische vermaning; 'Legt niemand haastelijk de handen op.'"

CHAPTER 7

Persecution at Home

Back in the province of Groningen, young Vander Werp, full of fire, fueled the flames of secession not only by preaching separation, but by writing about it as well. In 1835 he published two booklets: *Ode by a God-formed Patient and Meek Sufferer* and *Spiritual War Cry and Confession of my Faith on the Occasion of the Oppression and Persecution of H. de Cock*.[1]

This second booklet, written about the persecution of De Cock, contains thirty statements of his faith. Number 25 gives an indication as to why those who opposed Vander Werp believed he was a threat to the institutional church. It reads,

> I believe that it is the duty of every true believer to separate him or herself from the church of today, to regard this church as a Synagogue of Satan, where free will rules while many of its churches are filled with the darkness and smoke of every kind of heresy and error, and to join the true church wherever it may gather, because of persecution.[2]

---

[1]   D. J. Vander Werp. *Lofdicht van een door God geduldig en lijdzaam gemaakten lijder en Geestelijke Wapenkreten en Belijdenis mijns geloofs bij het verdrukken en vervolgen van H. de Cock* (Veendam, Mulder, 1835).

[2]   Wesseling, *Groningenland*, 1: 115. "Ik geloof, dat ieder ware gelovige verplicht is zich van de hedendaaagse kerk af te scheiden, als zijnde een Synagoge des Satans, omdat de vrije wil overal op de troon is, en vele kerken opgevuld zijn met rook en duisternis van allerlei ketterij en dwaling, en zich bij de ware kerk, waar die om vervolgzucht zich ook moet vergaderen, te voegen."

With that kind of rhetoric, it is understandable that in Groningen he experienced his share of persecution. For gathering and addressing a group of more than twenty, he was fined one hundred guilders with additional court costs. Because he could not afford such hefty fines, Vander Werp conducted many services in the countryside, away from meddling authorities. However, when found out, these services, too, were often disturbed. One Sunday men armed with clubs broke up a meeting; another time his opponents pelted Vander Werp with apples.

His popularity as a preacher among those dissatisfied with the Reformed Church was verified by Mayor H. B. Jonker to the governor of the province, in a letter dated September 14, 1835, in which he stated, "The services conducted by Douwe van der Werp, now living in this area, have taken place twice every Sunday, nearly the entire summer. They have taken place in the open air, and have been attended by large crowds of people coming from all directions in this province."[3]

As his popularity grew, he was also frequently asked to speak at funerals.[4] Because the Synod of Dort considers funerals family affairs, they were conducted from the home of the deceased.[5] The family's pastor would be invited to speak words of comfort at the home. However, it seemed that more than a few families preferred to engage Vander Werp during their time of grief rather than the local pastor.

Vander Werp's labors in the province that summer bore fruit. Each time De Cock made a trip to the province, he found groups ready to be organized. By early September seven churches had signed the Act of Secession (Wildervank, Stadskanaal, Veendam, Grootegast, Saaksum, Onstwedde, and Sappemeer). In September ten more joined in a matter of fourteen days.[6] While the authorities, unable to stem the tide, kept a wary eye on the state of affairs, those opposed to this wave of what they considered fanaticism began to fulminate against it.

News of De Cock's arrival at the home of baker Schuringa in Middelstum September 19 to formally organize a Secessionist

---

[3] Ibid., 2: 146. "De oefeningen door Douwe van der Werp thans te dezer plaatse woonachtig, hebben bijna de gehele zomer des zondags twee malen plaats gehad. En wel in het open veld ten aanhoren van een grote menigte mensen, uit alle oorden dezer provincie komende."

[4] Wesseling, *Groningerland*, 1: 137.

[5] The custom of conducting the funeral service in the home of the deceased lasted well into the mid twentieth century in the Netherlands, and among many Christian Reformed Church members in America as well.

[6] Appingedam, Delfzijl, 't Zandt, Middelstum, Westerwijtwerd, Uithuizen, Uithuizermeeden, Warffum, Spijk, and Thesinge.

Farm of Klaas Kremer in Uithuizen where De Cock
organized the Seceder Church in Uithuizen

congregation roused the opposition into action. Outside a large, seething crowd pelted the Schuringa home with stones, breaking windows and screaming obscenities at the small gathering inside. When finally Mayor Plaat arrived on the scene, he rebuked the perpetrators sternly, and told them to disband, yet he fined none of them.[7]

But the harassment Vander Werp and De Cock had experienced thus far was minor compared to what was waiting for them in Uithuizen, Vander Werp's hometown, two days later.[8]

Monday, September 21, 1835, De Cock preached at the farm of Klaas Kremer, situated just outside Uithuizen. After the service he formally organized the congregation. During the process of installing the elected elders and deacons for the new congregation, an irate crowd had gathered outside the house. Soon it broke through the doors and surged inside. De Cock, along with other congregants, fled through the back door and ran to Uithuizen amidst a barrage of shoves, punches, and angry shouts from the mob. On the way to his host, the town's miller, De Cock was thrown to the ground and pushed into a hedge.

---

[7]   J. F. Van Hulsteijn, *De Gereformeerde Kerk te Middelstum 1835-1935* (Middelstum: Gereformeerde Kerk, 1935), 31.

[8]   Wesseling, *Groningerland*, 1: 147. Even before De Cock came to Uithuizen to organize an *Afgescheiden* church, there had been trouble. A Frisian lay preacher and peddler in religious books led a service at the home of Derk Jans van der Kraak, teaching from the Heidelberg Catechism. The consistory of the Hervormde Kerk of Uithuizen brought complaints regarding this meeting to the court at Appingedam, which in turn fined Van der Kraak.

Losing his hat and one shoe, he ran to Bierma's bakery, where he thought he would be safe. But the furious, and by now out-of-control, crowd pushed its way into the baker's home as well. Someone wanted to extinguish the lamp so that his pursuers could assault De Cock without witnesses, but Bierma managed to stop them. Finally the mayor stepped in and under military escort led De Cock to his own home for safety. Uithuizen's uncivil behavior toward De Cock and the Seceders reflected the attitude of many at the time, and, again, no one was fined or held accountable.[9]

This particularly violent episode involving his former friends and neighbors must have grieved Vander Werp sorely. Nevertheless, these harassments did not keep him from preaching the Word, nor did it keep De Cock from organizing other congregations. The very next day, September 22, 1835, the Seceders in Uithuizermeeden formally organized. Fortunately, this event happened without incident. The newly formed congregation engaged Vander Werp as their regular lay pastor at an annual salary of 450 guilders.[10] As president of the consistory, Vander Werp was, at age twenty-four, by far its youngest member. Leading a congregation at his age, and without formal theological education testified to his gifts of leadership, administration, and preaching. He earned his keep. Each Sunday he preached three times, as well as many times during the week. In a letter to the king requesting permission to organize, he claimed to have five hundred souls in the congregation—an impressive number for a young lay pastor.

Johannes Damsté, pastor of the Reformed Church in Uithuizermeeden at the time, found this figure highly inflated. In a letter to the minister of worship he wrote,

> Fifty-six actual confessing members have taken their membership out of my church. The rest number about one hundred and fifty attendees, counting the children. I have even heard that some of these are already regretting that they signed up with De Cock and Vander Werp. If you can stop this Douwe Vander Werp from preaching, these troubles and this unrest will stop; otherwise, I am afraid that they will only continue to increase.[11]

---

[9]   Wesseling, *Groningerland*, 1: 154-56.

[10] On August 3, 1835, he preached his inaugural sermon on 1 Peter 5:10, 11.

[11] Wesseling, *Groningerland*, 2: 146-48. "Slechts 56 belijdende leden zouden bij hem niet meer in de kerk komen, maar in particuliere huizen vergaderen, terwijl hij mischien 150 'onderhorige leken' (bijwoonders) en kinderen meende te kunnen

No doubt Vander Werp must have felt a certain amount of vindication for having been dismissed from his teaching position; now only one year later, he was the lay pastor of a sizable congregation. Like Joseph of old, he probably reasoned that Hofstede de Groot had meant it to humble him, but the Lord had meant it for good. Nevertheless, in another year, Vander Werp would also know the Lord's hand against him in a very painful and personal way.

tellen. Terwijl ik zelfs nu en dan hoor dat het reeds sommigen berouwt hun namen voor H. de Cock en D. van der Werp getekend te hebben. Indien Douwe van der Werp het oefenen kon worden verboden of belet, dan zouden de ongeregeldheden verminderen, terwijl het anders te vrezen staat, dat ze hoe langer hoe meer zullen toenemen."

CHAPTER 8

Marriage and Ordination

The portrayal of the Seceders as belonging to the poor and lower class people is only partly correct. There were many well to do among them who gave unstintingly of their material goods to the cause, especially by making their homes available as meeting places.

Both the Uithuizen and Uithuizermeeden congregations had some wealthy members in their midst. One family, the Van Dams, members of Uithuizermeeden, were *landbouwers* or farmers, and fiercely secession-minded. In February 1835, Harm Van Dam, sixty-two at the time, was fined one hundred guilders, plus another eight guilders in court costs, for having a worship service in his home. Two days later his son, twenty-seven year old Jacob, was fined the same amount for the same reason.

Vander Werp was well acquainted with the Van Dam family, since he was courting their daughter, Martje. Part of their courtship centered on attending conventicles.[1] In Martje, he had found a soul mate, one as committed to the secessionist cause as he was. They were married November 7, 1835; Vander Werp was twenty-four and Martje was twenty-five years old at the time.

In the Netherlands, even today, marriages are considered legally binding only when performed by a civil magistrate in a ceremony at a

---

[1] Wesseling, *Groningerland*, 2: 40. Their names were on a list attending a clandestine worship service led by De Cock September 11, 1835, in the home of Jacobus Klok of Delfzijl.

city hall or county courthouse. If people wish to have their marriage also solemnized in a church service that is their decision. The Seceders highly recommended the latter, and in all likelihood De Cock officiated at the church wedding of Vander Werp and Martje. Whatever feelings the Vander Werps had regarding their eldest son's church affiliation, the family bonds were still such that they were present at the wedding and gave their consent. Jan Hendrik acted as a witness for his brother.[2]

For the time being, the young couple moved in with Martje's parents. The large farmhouse of the Van Dams comfortably housed father and mother Van Dam, their sons Remmert and Lammert, their daughter Reina, with her husband and their two children, two live-in maids, and the Vander Werps.[3]

The winter of 1835 began with a stretch of very cold weather in early November. The day after Douwe and Martje married, a heavy snowfall brought all traffic to a halt for several days.[4] During the remainder of the winter, without any further major storms, Vander Werp managed to keep up his preaching and teaching schedule in the area around Uithuizermeeden, while De Cock traveled throughout the province of Friesland to organize Secessionist congregations.[5]

In November two more pastors left the Reformed Church and formally declared themselves *Afgescheiden*: Anthony Brummelkamp on November 21, and George Frans Gezelle Meerburg on November 24. Less than a month later, on December 11, Simon Van Velzen joined the movement. This eased the burden on De Cock to some degree, yet the increasing number of Secessionist congregations led to an ever-increasing dependence on the use of lay preachers. This was not a satisfactory situation, since many of them did not have any theological training. While most had some grade school education, a few could not even write.[6] The lack of systematic theological training led to a diversity of teaching, since each lay preacher preached as he felt led by the Spirit. Many were suspected of being led not by the Holy Spirit, but by their

---

[2]   Civil Registry of Marriages Municipality of Uithuizermeeden, Groningen, the Netherlands. Salt Lake City, Utah, Family History Library International Film #109,607.

[3]   Wesseling, *Groningerland*, 1: 115.

[4]   J. Buisman, *Bar en Boos, Zeven eeuwen winterweer in de lage landen* (Baarn: Bosch & Keuning, 1984), 200-201.

[5]   Wesseling, *Friesland*, 1: 13, 21.

[6]   Wesseling, *Friesland*, 1: 30. For instance, Pieter Kornelis Radema, lay preacher in Burum, Friesland, could not write; however, that did not mean these people were illiterate—many had been taught to read but not to write.

Lijnbaangracht 198,
Amsterdam, where the first
Seceder synod convened in
1836

own pride and a desire for attention, and of causing unrest with their inflammatory rhetoric.[7]

As a married man and increasingly respected leader in the Secessionist movement, Vander Werp's hope of becoming a fully ordained minister now rested with the decision of the movement's first synod which met March 2, 1836. Five *Afgescheiden* pastors and eleven elders met in the home of Van Velzen's mother-in-law on the Lijnbaansgracht in Amsterdam.[8] One of the items on their agenda dealt with the ordination of lay preachers.

---

[7]   S. Van Velzen, "Brief van eenen leeraar aan de Christelijke Gereformeerde Gemeente in Nederland." *De Reformatie*, 3: 336-58. The situation worsened to such an extent that in 1838 Simon Van Velzen, in an article in the *De Reformatie*, strongly urged that no untrained pastors be allowed to shepherd a congregation. Or, in the event they were chosen, to refrain from preaching themselves, but instead to read a sermon prepared by an ordained minister.

[8]   Algra, *Wonder*, 128. The first session of this first synod dealt with a response to the king's declaration of December 11, 1835 that the *Afgescheiden* were not given permission to form their own churches. In spite of the Constitution of the Netherlands, which guaranteed freedom of religion, the king had reminded the

Vander Werp awaited the outcome with great eagerness. The synod's decision regarding the ordination of lay preachers in the face of the acute shortage of trained clergy could open the way for him to become an ordained pastor before long. As soon as the news reached Vander Werp that De Cock had returned from Amsterdam, he hurried to hear all that was said and done.

De Cock knew what Vander Werp most wanted to hear. Were the brethren amenable to his ordination? He tried to break the news to his friend gently. The synod, he told him, had decided not to ordain lay preachers without proper theological training. Even lay preachers, De Cock explained, would have to be formally called by a congregation and undergo a rigorous classical examination.

Vander Werp's deep disappointment about the matter had a personal aspect. By now his relationship with De Cock was such that he did not hesitate to share his feelings. Martje was expecting, and together they had fervently hoped and prayed he might be ordained so that he could administer the sacrament of baptism to their first child.[9]

De Cock could only comfort the young couple by promising them he would gladly administer the sacrament himself.[10] He encouraged Vander Werp to consider theological training like other lay leaders who had decided to go that route. De Cock would train him personally. Nevertheless, Vander Werp held back. There was the time and the expense to consider now that he had a wife and child. He could not expect financial support from his in-laws—the Van Dams valued

delegation that the Constitution said "freedom to *bestaande* [existing] groups, and not freedom to [form] new groups. If they persisted in forming a new denomination, they had to remember to stipulate in their constitution that they would not be able to receive any financial aid from the government for the upkeep of their buildings or support of their pastors, that they were not out to create public unrest, and that they were to renounce any say in property belonging to the Dutch Reformed Church. They could not be guaranteed any safeguards from the government. It was these pronouncements that had led directly to the formation of the first synod, in which the *Afgescheiden* wanted to address the king and to set guidelines for the newly formed denomination.

9   Keizer, *Afscheiding*, 94. The letter Scholte wrote back to De Cock in which he cautions De Cock against ordaining Vander Werp mentions specifically that Vander Werp could preach all he wanted to, but that De Cock should do the baptizing, indicating some desire on Vander Werp's part to baptize.

10 Johannes, born August 28, 1836 was not baptized until June 18, 1837, presumably by De Cock since there were no other ordained *Afgescheiden* ministers in the area.

spiritual gifts more highly than theological training.[11] Consequently he decided to continue to work as a lay pastor for the time being.

At home, his happiness over the birth of baby Johannes, born August 28, 1836, was overshadowed by his concern for Martje's health. She never recovered from childbirth and died in December of that same year. Later, Vander Werp would often mention to his friends how on her deathbed she had prophesied that during his life, he would see Zion grow.[12] Martje's prophecy about Zion's growth was based on Psalm 128, a favorite psalm of Christian young married couples. Realizing that she would not be the mother of many children around their table, she nevertheless claimed the promise for Douwe, that if he stayed faithful, the promise of "seeing Zion grow and Jerusalem prosper" would still be his.

Stricken by grief, he nevertheless decided to honor his wife's memory by working hard to make "Zion" grow. In order to accomplish this, he left little Johannes in the capable care of his sister-in-law, Reina Van Dam, and traveled throughout the province, preaching to groups interested in secession and, when invited, staying in the home of a fellow believer. After a short January thaw in 1837, freezing temperatures, snow, and sleet hampered travel through much of February, March, and April.[13] On March 17, Vander Werp, in a letter bringing De Cock up to date on the conditions regarding persecution, wrote:

> It is limited and kept to a small number, except in Kropswolde, where Huisken was to preach on Tuesday but was prevented because the so-called pastor had previously persuaded the mayor of Hoogezand to persecute him.

The health situation seemed worse than the persecution; he wrote:

> Not only are entire families ill, but almost entire villages have had colds and a type of flu, which causes fever, severe body pains, congestion in the chest, light-headedness, and swollen eyes. [14]

---

[11] This is evidenced by the fact that Wolter van Dam, Martje's brother, exhorted for years as a lay preacher, without seeking theological education and ordination.

[12] "Levens-beschrijving bij het portret van D. J. Vander Werp." *Christian Reformed Church Yearbook* 1892, 51-52.

[13] Buisman, *Bar,* 201.

[14] D. Hellema, *Kroniek van een Friese Boer* (Franeker: Wever, 1978), 214: Hellema describes this flu as follows: "In our entire fatherland and also in our area, in the cities and in the country there is for a considerable time now a very contagious illness which people call the flu. In Leeuwarden many have died."

Vander Werp, who was staying with the Alkemas at the time, continued:

> Alkema's wife and children are somewhat ill; the maid is very sick. I was also affected quite a bit so that I had to remain here for some time, but now I am improving somewhat. Alkema, his wife and the congregation would be pleased to hear about your circumstances, and the affairs of the church. If the Lord wills and we live, they would feel honored and pleased to have you come as soon as He opens the way.[15]

In the letter Vander Werp also passed on a recipe to De Cock, who apparently suffered from ulcers on his legs:

> Take the root of a dandelion [he wrote], and steep it in water. Use this water to wash the wounds. Purchase five cents worth of [oil of] basilicum in which to dip the dressing before putting it on the wounds. In between dressings, continue to wash the wounds with the dandelion root water. After several days of this treatment, with God's blessing, healing should take place.[16]

During the summer that followed, both De Cock and Vander Werp continued to be engaged actively in the work of the church. In June they met in Uithuizermeeden and little Johannes was baptized along with Reina's children. Just when it seemed there were solid signs of growth among the *Afgescheiden*, and that the Lord was blessing the Secession, the first crack appeared, leaving a trail of shattered relationships, even friendships, for years to come.

Meeting from September 28, 1837, to October 11, 1837, the second synod, presided over by Simon Van Velzen, adopted a new church order based on the Church Order of Dort, but with some modifications, taking the times into consideration.[17] A number of

---

[15]   Vander Werp Collection, Calvin College Archives, letter Vander Werp to De Cock.

[16]   Ibid.

[17]   *Handelingen en Verslagen van de Algemene Synoden van de Christelijk Afgescheidene Gereformeerde Kerk (1836-1869)* (Houten/Utrecht: Den Hartog, 1984), 73-176. The National Synod of the *Afgescheiden* met from September 28 to October 11, 1837. This synod reviewed carefully each of the articles of the Synod of Dort, forty-two articles were modified, eight were deleted, and thirty-six were accepted without change. H. Scholte, who had written the draft of the new church order, heavily influenced the acceptance of these changes and the resulting church order became known as the Church

congregations, mostly from the northern provinces and led by De Cock, resisted these changes with the result that they seceded—the first split from the Seceders. Another difference with the *Afgescheiden* was their stance of not wishing to petition the Dutch government for permission to organize as a church. They reasoned that they would then exist "under the authority of the government," rather than "under the cross" and began calling themselves *Kerken onder het Kruis* (*Kruisgezinden* for short), i.e. Churches under [the authority of] the Cross, as opposed to Churches under [the authority of] the State. This term had also been given to persecuted churches by the Reformers at the beginning of the Reformation. In 1869 the Dutch government finally relented and allowed any group desiring to form an ecclesiastical community to have that right without requiring government approval.

The *Kruisgezinden* adopted the original Dortian Church Order without any changes. Following De Cock's lead, Vander Werp also joined this group. A sizable number joining these *Kruisgezinden*, including Vander Werp's brother, Jan Hendrik, came from Uithuizermeeden and Bierum, two communities in the northern part of the province of Groningen.[18]

The Reverend Albertus C. Van Raalte, one of the Secessionist ministers who had been in favor of modifying the church rules, made a hasty trip north to persuade De Cock to come back to the Secessionist group.[19] De Cock followed Van Raalte's advice, leaving Vander Werp in a quandary. Should he go back with De Cock, or stay with the *Kruisgezinden*? His father-in-law, Harm van Dam, and his brother-in-law, Wolter van Dam, were members of the group. Wolter, also a lay preacher, had been exhorting far and wide in the area. He had left the Reformed Church in favor of De Cock, but at one point the two differed; when De Cock censured him for abusing his office as elder, Wolter and his father went over to the *Kruisgezinden* and continued preaching.[20] No doubt, these highly intense in-laws exerted pressure on Vander Werp to

Order of Utrecht. De Cock and the northern group could not agree to these changes believing that any deviation from the original set forth by the Synod of Dort (1618-1619) would negate their ability to say they were not seceding, but returning to the original church order and doctrines.

[18]   Wesseling, *Groningerland*, 1: 151.

[19]   Bouwman, *Crisis*, 27. Albertus C. Van Raalte (1811-1876) immigrated to America in 1847 with a sizable group of followers. Vander Werp and Van Raalte were born in the same year in the Netherlands and passed away in the same year, 1876, in Michigan.

[20]   Wesseling, *Groningerland*, 3: 296, 306-307.

side with them. Also, he may have felt beholden to them because, even though Martje had passed away, he and little Johannes were still living in the Van Dam home.

The *Kruisgezinden* were in a quandary as well. With De Cock gone back to the main body, they were left without an ordained pastor to perform the sacraments. For nearly three years, these *Kruisgezinden* met without regular observance of the Lord Supper or having their children baptized.[21] During those three years, Vander Werp worked in their midst.

Desperate for ordained pastors, they held a meeting June 11, 1840, in Mastenbroek, province of Overijssel, during which a motion was passed to ordain several lay pastors to clergy status, including Vander Werp. There was some discussion regarding examination of the candidates but that was set aside; the motion to do so did not carry. Although Vander Werp presided at this meeting, it must not be construed that he had any part in the plan that took place the following Sunday. Van der Does states that "even those ordained knew nothing of the plan."[22] The evening before, A. Schouwenberg, one of the elders, had warned another elder in secret "to be ready for something out of the ordinary."[23] In a church service held at the home of A. Ridderinkhoff in Zwolle, Sunday, June 14, 1840, Schouwenberg ordained W. W. Smitt and Vander Werp. In the evening service, Smitt ordained Schouwenberg. Many in the congregation could not justify these actions and walked out. Their leaders had insisted upon strict adherence to the original Church Order of Dort only to ignore it when it did not suit their purpose.[24]

Deeply troubled by what had taken place, Vander Werp agonized over the validity of his ordination, since it had none of the prerequisites required by the Church Order of Dort. These stated that in order for a person to be ordained to the ministry, he had to pass a rigorous classical examination and be called by a specific congregation. Vander Werp's knowledge of the Church Order—which he had defended vigorously

---

[21]   Because marriages were not considered a sacrament, elders were allowed to solemnize marriages.

[22]   J. C. van der Does, *Kruisgezinden en Separatisten* (Franeker: Wever, 1940), 45.

[23]   A. Schouwenberg (1789-1854).

[24]   As a rationale for their action, the *Kruisgezinde* elders stated that the *Afgescheiden* pastors had all been ordained originally by clergy of the Reformed Church which they (and De Cock) considered the "false" church, so how could these Reformed clergy be more sanctioned to ordain *Afgescheiden* clergy than an elder from the "true church"?

thus far—helped him see his lapse in judgment. By week's end he had recanted his hasty act. It is not sure at what point he returned to the *Afgescheiden*, but in November of that same year the Synod of Amsterdam rescinded the changes made to the Dortian Church Order in 1837.[25] It may be that this action (which had spawned the secession of the *Kruisgezinden*) helped Vander Werp justify his return to them. Sometime between June and November of 1840 he turned to his old friend and previous mentor, De Cock, to begin his training for the ministry.

---

[25] *Handelingen en Verslagen* (1836-1869), meeting in Amsterdam from November 17 to December 3, 1840, Articles 5-13. At this same synod, Articles 14-15, Scholte is reprimanded for, among others, his divisive writing in *De Reformatie* and subsequently deposed for not accepting the original Church Order of Dort, 246-47.

CHAPTER 9

Studying with De Cock

A much chastened and more mature Vander Werp presented himself at De Cock's doorstep. The events of the last two years must have alternately perplexed, infuriated, and disheartened him. It was one thing to rant and rave against those who were clearly against the seceders and their cause; it was another thing to fight within the movement in those same strident tones.[1] If they were all filled with the Holy Spirit, why was there so much disunity? Were there, perhaps, also some sinful personality traits rearing their ugly heads? Had their zeal for the true church been stained with the zeal of their own importance? Had he not also been guilty of pushing his own agenda by declaring who was and who was not a true member of the church? He realized that the time had come for him to listen and learn.

De Cock received his young friend warmly. He had settled in the city of Groningen and had been training lay pastors to prepare them for ministry.[2] After the two had sorted out their differences, De Cock declared his willingness to help Vander Werp achieve his goal. Twice a week he was to join several other students at De Cock's home on Guldenstraat.[3]

[1] *Handeling en Verslagen*, 79. In the introduction to the published synodical proceedings, Van Velzen wrote that anyone not accepting the changes to the Church Order would be considered schismatic, would put themselves under God's curse, and suffer the same fate as Korah, Dathan, and Abiram in the Old Testament.
[2] In Drenthe, F.A. Kok, and farther south, A. Brummelkamp, were training men for ministry.
[3] Wesseling, *Afscheiding en Doleantie in de Stad Groningen* (Groningen: Niemeijer, 1961), 41.

House in Groningen where first De Cock and later De Haan instructed Vander Werp

Besides Bible knowledge, the curriculum included a study of theology, church history, geography of Bible lands, and preaching. Because the need for pastors had reached a critical stage, some criteria, such as learning Greek and Hebrew, were eliminated for those who did not have university training.[4]

Much had happened in the years Vander Werp had spent with the Kruisgezinden. The number of Secessionist congregations had grown dramatically. King William I, who had tried to halt their spread with heavy-handed tactics, had abdicated in favor of his son, King William II. De Cock, with three fellow clergy, had met with this new king shortly after the Synod of 1840, held in Amsterdam.[5] At the advice of his cabinet ministers, the new king had ceased the persecution of the Seceders, allowing them freedom of worship. However, on the matter of Christian education for their children, the Seceders still met stiff resistance from the government. Since the education law of 1806 forbade the teaching of the Heidelberg Catechism in the schools and the schools had become more and more secularized, De Cock counseled the Seceders to keep the children out of school. He also counseled consistories to insist on having Christian schools to help parents keep their baptismal vow to do everything to the utmost of their ability to

[4] The first synod had stated that in times of need, the church could ordain pastors who had not studied Greek and Hebrew. See also L. Praamsma, *Het dwaze Gods* (Wageningen: Zomer & Keuning), 124.

[5] Wormser, *Werken*, 154. Brummelkamp, De Cock, Van Velzen, and Dijksterhuis.

have their child instructed in the doctrines of the church. He based his advice on Article 21 of the Church Order of Dort, which stated that it was the duty of each consistory to see to it that in addition to the usual subjects, teachers must also instruct in the Heidelberg Catechism.[6] Many Seceders followed De Cock's example and kept their children out of school, leading to a generation in which many church members had poor reading skills, and in many cases were unable to write.

During this time Vander Werp also made some changes in his living arrangements. Since his break with the Kruisgezinden, he had become uncomfortable living with the Van Dams, choosing instead to move to Sappemeer to work among the Seceders there. He had worked in this area in the spring of 1837 and knew many of the people. Sappemeer, located east of the city of Groningen, enjoyed a certain economic prosperity due to its location on the Winschoterdiep waterway and the traffic that moved along it. For Vander Werp the waterway provided an easy means of getting in and out of Groningen a couple of times a week for his classes.

Occasionally on his trips into Groningen, Vander Werp may have made a slight detour through the Grote Markt, to Roelof Schierbeek's or Willem Zuidema's book dealership, but surely to Schildkamp's on Oude Boteringstraat because the latter carried many of De Cock's publications.[7] Because there were no bookstores outside of Groningen, anyone wanting or needing any kind of book, pamphlet, or other printed material had to come to the city. Local schoolteachers and traveling peddlers were the usual sources of literature in the countryside.[8] The Dutch were a literate people and loved reading. By mid century there were over one hundred reading clubs in the province of Groningen alone. Travel accounts, adventure stories, and biographies were especially popular. American Revolutionary heroes, such as George Washington and Benjamin Franklin, enjoyed wide admiration.[9]

At other times, Vander Werp would stop at the newly opened tobacco shop of Theodorus Niemeyer, for a supply of pipe tobacco for

---

[6]   Article 21 of the Church Order of Dort states, "De Kerkeraden zullen alomme toezien, dat er goede schoolmeesters zijn, die niet alleen de kinderen leeren lezen, schrijven, spreken en vrije kunsten, maar ook dezelve in de godzaligheid en in den Catechismus onderwijzen."

[7]   Keizer, *Afscheiding van 1834*, 39.

[8]   IJ. Botke, *Gaat, krijgt een boek of pen in hant en oefent daarin Uw verstant* (Groningen: Universiteits-bibliotheek, 1988), 93-95.

[9]   Ibid., 36.

Tamme F. De Haan

De Cock, his fellow students, and himself. [10] Then, settling down with a lit pipe in a room filled with smoke, the students listened as De Cock lectured.

Smoking had enjoyed a long and honored tradition in the Netherlands. Pipe and cigar smoking were commonplace and chewing tobacco so habitual that even churches had spittoons. Among the male population, a nonsmoker was an oddity. By the time they were eight to ten years of age, young boys were encouraged to smoke.[11]

---

[10]   Wesseling, *Groningerland*, 2: 156. Mayor C. Hartman Busman in his report to the Governor stated that the policeman sent out to check on De Cock's whereabouts in Sappemeer found him in the home of Kars F. Wormnest, sitting and smoking with others.

[11]   Wouter van Riesen, "Eene Friesche vrijage uit Napoleon's dagen," *Stemmen des Tijds Maandschrift voor Christendom en Cultuur*, W. J. Aalders, et al. eds. (Zeist: Ruys' Uitgevers-Mij, 1929), 18, 193-212. "Want het overmatig rooken van tabak was in die dagen een nationaal gebruik geworden en het was zeldzaam een man van welken stand ook zonder pijp in den mond, of zonder tondeldoos en vuurslag te zien. Het rooken gold voor nuttig niet alleen, maar noodig tegen de vochtige luchtsgesteldheid; jongens van acht tot tien jaar werden er toe aangezet."

Grave marker of the
Rev. H. De Cock

People smoked everywhere, at home, at the office, in the shops and inns, in stagecoaches, on barges, and sometimes even in church.[12] The consistory meetings of the Afgescheiden congregation of Groningen were held in a room on the second floor in De Cock's home. While the members had to contribute five cents for coffee, De Cock was reimbursed forty guilders per year for rental of the room, heating the stove, and supplying pipes and tobacco.[13] Ministers were advised to take

[12] Paul Zumthor, *Daily Life in Rembrandt's Holland*, trans. S. W. Taylor (Stanford: Stanford Univ. Press, 1994), 179.

[13] J. Wesseling, *Afscheiding en Doleantie in de Stad Groningen* (Groningen: Niemeijer, 1961), 41. See also Wim Schrijver, "Kerk Donkerbroek betaalde tabak voor de kerkeraad," at www.leeuwarder-courant.nl/PaginaPrint/ 1,7159,23-7-4921-5579-931434---,00.html (January 19, 2003). In the *Afgescheiden* Church of Donkerbroek, Friesland, the consistory members charged their pipes and tobacco to the church.

along a good cigar when visiting the sick and poor so that their odors were offset by the smell of the cigar.[14]

And even though it stained their teeth and fouled their breath, no one considered smoking a health risk, least of all Vander Werp. His thoughts were directed to his studies, his work, and lately to courting a young woman in Sappemeer—Albertje Boersma, the daughter of farmer Reinder Boersma. By now Vander Werp had been a widower for more than three years, and remarrying and making a home for his son, Johannes, seemed to be a real and happy possibility.

The only bleak spot at this time was the continued concern over the state of De Cock's health. The years of stress, persecution, and constant travel had taken their toll. As a consequence of his opposition to smallpox vaccination, the entire De Cock family had been ill with the disease.[15] De Cock's health deteriorated rapidly. By the end of the summer he could no longer meet with his students. The news spread rapidly among the Seceders, how, while preaching one Sunday in September, he began spitting up blood. On November 14, 1842, at age forty-one, Hendrik De Cock passed from the church militant to the church triumphant.

Vander Werp, who served as a pallbearer with the other students, stood at the gravesite and grieved along with all those who had dearly loved De Cock.[16] God, he knew, was not to be questioned. Nevertheless, he must have wondered why a man like De Cock, who had done so much for the kingdom, and, given life, could still do so much more, should die so young. Even so, in his mourning Vander Werp honored the wishes of De Cock's widow who asked her fellow mourners to accept the Lord's will in this matter.[17]

Although De Cock's death curtailed Vander Werp's education for a while, he was able to continue his studies when Tamme F. De Haan was appointed March 20, 1843, to fill the vacancy left by De Cock.[18] De

---

[14]   C. E. van Koetsveld, *Schetsen uit de Pastorie te Mastland, Ernst en Luim uit het leven van den Nederlandschen dorpsleeraar*, 7th ed. (Schoonhoven: Van Nooten, 1874), 167.

[15]   J. A. Wormser, *Werken zoolang het dag is: Het leven van Hendrik de Cock* (Nijverdal: E. J. Bosch, 1915), 155.

[16]   Wesseling, *Stad Groningen*, 49.

[17]   Ibid., 49.

[18]   J. de Haas, *Gedenkt Uw Voorgangers*, 5 vols. (Haarlem: Vijlbrief, 1984), 1:131. Tamme Foppes de Haan (1791-1868) joined the Secessionist movement while pastor at Ee in Friesland. Because he preferred teaching to preaching, he began training students for the ministry in Leeuwarden, then took over De Cock's work in Groningen in

Haan had been training young men for the ministry in Friesland and was acquainted with the needs of the congregations in that province. Apparently he was sufficiently impressed with Vander Werp's gifts for ministry that when the Secesionist congregation of Leeuwarden asked him to recommend a pastor, he recommended Vander Werp. Vander Werp, eager to give up the itinerant preacher's life, gladly accepted the opportunity. In August 1843 he moved to Leeuwarden to begin his ministry as student-pastor.[19] His experience and knowledge would soon be put to the test.

1843, and became one of the first professors at the theological school in Kampen in 1854.

[19]   Wesseling, *Friesland,* 2: 241.

CHAPTER 10

Leeuwarden and Ordination

Until this time Vander Werp had worked mostly with people in Groningen and Drenthe—two provinces whose people and language were different from that of the people of Friesland. The Frisians are known for their fiercely independent streak, which shows up in their church history as well. While the Synod of Dort had recommended that its three forms of unity be accepted by all the Reformed churches in the Seven United Provinces, the Frisian Provincial Synod had never demanded of any minister serving a Frisian church that he sign the form of subscription.[1] Most of the clergy in Friesland had been trained at the University of Groningen, and had embraced the theologically liberal Groninger *Richting*, or Direction. De Cock estimated that there were only twelve theologically conservative ministers in all of Friesland in 1834.[2]

There were other signs of spiritual laxity. By 1820, a decade after the civil code no longer recognized ecclesiastical marriages as legally binding, but only those performed before a civil court, church

---

[1] Rudolf J. Staverman, *Buitenkerkelijk in Friesland* (Assen: Van Gorcum,1954), 82. See also Rienk Klooster, *Groninger Godgeleerheid in Friesland 1830-1872* (Leeuwarden, Netherlands, Fryske Akademy, 2001), 384.

[2] Wesseling, *Friesland*, 1: 20. They were Arie Van Velden, Jan Mangel, Pieter Dirks Koopman, Theunis Van Berkum, Arnoldus E. Buning, Simon Hogerzeil, Jan Lamberts, Lucas Fockens, Jan Willem Becking, Laurens Van Loon, Tamme Foppens De Haan, and Jan Rudolph De Bruine.

Leeuwarden, Friesland, 1700s city scene

solemnization of marriages in Friesland declined dramatically.[3] The court required those wishing to marry to present proper documentation, but it did not consider premarital sex an issue, and many couples often were expectant parents by the time they reached the courthouse. Seceders, on the other hand, recommended strongly that couples begin their married life with God's blessing in a church setting. They frowned on premarital sexual behavior, considered it a transgression of the seventh commandment, and required a public confession of the brother and sister who had fallen into this sin.[4] The courts as servants of the state did not make the religious affiliation of the intended bride and groom an issue either. The Seceders, however, felt that a couple "should not be unequally yoked," and that interfaith marriages should

[3]   Ibid., 79. The church report of 1819 stated that Friesland was not the only province dealing with the scarcity of church marriages. See also Marang, *Zwijndrechtsche Nieuwlichters*, 139. "Classis Dordrecht 1843: Ten aanzien van de kerkelijke inzegening des huwelijks was het treurig gesteld. Enkele voorbeelden geeft het rapport van 1846: Te Hendrik-Ido-Ambacht werden in 15 jaar tijds slechts 5 huwelijken ingezegend; te Oud-Beijerland 6 in 16 jaar; te Heinenoord in 11 jaar niet een; te Klaaswaal 1 in 16 jaar." See also Pereboom, *Scheurmakers*, 66.

[4]   The subject of church marriages was addressed by the first synod held in 1836 in Amsterdam; Article 36.

Leeuwarden, Friesland, 1800s city scene

be avoided.[5] This wholesale drop-off in church marriages reflected the general public's low regard for the institutional church. In order to draw couples back to church for a Christian ceremony, some churches allowed an "extra" service on the same day as the civil wedding, so that couples did not have to wait until the following Sunday to have their marriage solemnized by the church.[6]

Secularly, Leeuwarden—a town of 19,000 residents—was a garrison town, a *kermis* or carnival town, and a market town that regularly attracted all kinds of people from the entire province. At any one time, boats from all over the province moored in the city's canals, loading and unloading cargo. There were theaters and music halls for entertainment and plenty of cafes and drinking establishments. The many soldiers stationed in Leeuwarden attracted numerous prostitutes. In 1823 there were between thirty and forty houses of prostitution. And, although prostitution was not a criminal offense, the Seceders considered it an abomination. In short, there was plenty of opportunity for sin, and plenty of work for a young pastor.[7]

---

[5] For more on the marriage situation, see Van Weerden, *Spanningen*, 221-29, and S. J. Th. Homan, *Het ontstaan van de Gereformeerde Kerk te Leek* (Leek, Bronsema, 1986), 27.

[6] Pereboom, *Scheurmakers*, 66.

[7] Mathijsen, *Gemaskerde Eeuw*, 63-66. The regulation of prostitution began in 1811 with the introduction of the Napoleonic Code in the Netherlands, which was

Shortly before Vander Werp accepted the call to Leeuwarden, the congregation experienced a split, which reduced the number of members to a mere handful and led to the loss of its church building. Under the guidance of De Haan the members worked out their differences, found another building, and felt ready to call a new shepherd to lead them. When De Haan proposed his student as pastor, Vander Werp had not yet completed his studies for the ministry, and the people of Leeuwarden deemed it inappropriate for a student to mount the pulpit.

Wyger Doekes Hellema, a well-to-do and influential farmer, especially protested having an as yet unordained lay preacher as pastor.[8] Hellema had the support of the Reverend Van Velsen in this matter, and for the time being the pulpit was removed from the church and a lectern installed, so that when he exhorted, Vander Werp would be on an even footing with his parishioners. Pulpits in the Reformed churches were more than glorified lecterns, they were octagonal wooden structures, raised several feet from the floor and resting on a pedestal. The pulpit was entered by climbing a small stairway and closed with a door at the top of the stairs.[9] Above it hung a sounding board, so that the pastor could be heard as well as seen. The older pulpits were often elaborately carved with meaningful symbolism. The symbolism of the pulpit itself was that the Word of God was above the sacraments, in direct opposition to that of Roman Catholicism.

Not all members of the Leeuwarden congregation were happy with the removal of their pulpit; the matter came up at a classis meeting at which the delegates of Leeuwarden were asked why this had been done. They answered that it had been done simply for convenience and without any malicious intent.[10]

---

already in use in France. All prostitutes had to register with the police to stem the spread of venereal disease among the military. After the French retreat from the Netherlands this law was repealed, but William I saw the law's usefulness and urged municipalities to regulate prostitution in their areas. Prostitution was not considered a crime as long as it did not involve minors.

[8] Son of Doeke Wygers Hellema, author of *Kroniek van een Friese Boer* (Franeker: Wever, 1978).

[9] Wim Zaal, *God's onkruid, Nederlandse sekten en messiassen* (Masterdam: Meulenhoff, 1972), 10. Because these pulpits hid the minister's bottom half, they were often called a *houten broek,* or wooden pants.

[10] D. Deddens and J. Kamphuis, eds. *Afscheiding – Wederkeer: Opstellen over de Afscheiding van 1834* (Haarlem: Vijlbrief, 1984), 191.

It is doubtful whether the action of removing the pulpit by order of the church authorities bothered Vander Werp all that much. He had seen De Cock's reaction when barred from the Ulrum pulpit after having seceded. De Cock just climbed on a bench and preached anyway. It was the preaching that mattered, not the outward accoutrements. Even so, when the matter of pulpit versus lectern came up years later on the other side of the ocean in a classis meeting in Graafschap, Vander Werp voted in favor of the lectern for lay readers, reserving the pulpit for clergy only.[11]

With a firm commitment from his new congregation and an annual salary of eight hundred guilders, from which he had to supply his own lodgings, Vander Werp felt confident he could take on the responsibility of a new marriage.[12] He and Albertje Reinders Boersma, the farmer's daughter from Sappemeer, Groningen, were united in marriage in November 1843. They moved into a house on Wisserstraat, next to the church. After nearly seven years of sporadic separation, Vander Werp could finally bring his son, Johannes, home to live with him.

Early the following spring, Vander Werp's examination for the ministry took place in a combined meeting of the classes of Friesland, Groningen, and Drenthe, held in Leeuwarden. On Wednesday, March 20, 1844, and days following, twelve candidates presented themselves. Not only their knowledge but also their endurance would be put to the test. On Thursday the candidates were given texts on which they were to hand in a written sermon the next day. Friday morning the examinations continued. From nine a.m. to two p.m. the examination in languages took place, after which followed biblical exegesis and Bible history, which lasted for eight hours.[13] The day being far spent, the delegates decided to meet through the night. After a short intermission they

---

11   CRC Synod Minutes, September 1866, Art. 25
12   B. De Groot, "Douwe Johannes van der Werp, 1811-1876: Een Cocksiaan van het eerste uur, " *Jaarboek voor de geschiedenis van de Gereformeerde Kerken in Nederland,* no. 3, D. Th. Kuiper, ed. (Kampen: Kok, n.d.), 26. Reformed church pastors were earning salaries between one and two thousand guilders annually. *Afgescheiden* pastors were earning between five hundred and one thousand guilders, reflecting the economic status of their respective congregations.
13   Bouwman, *Crisis*, 65. The older students who had already served as lay preachers were excused from language studies. Since Vander Werp's training had not included the study of Latin, Greek, or Hebrew, he was excused from this part of the examination.

resumed at ten p.m. and examined the candidates regarding dogmatics until six o'clock in the morning. Then followed the examination in church history and geography of the Holy Land, after which they gave personal testimonies of their inner calling to the ministry.

After the examination, four of the candidates were found wanting.[14] Vander Werp belonged to those who passed. He then officially accepted the call extended to him by the congregation of Leeuwarden to become its pastor, and was formally ordained April 7, 1844, by De Haan. It is generally assumed that the pulpit was restored to the church at that time. What a satisfying moment it must have been for Vander Werp, at age thirty-three, to have finally achieved full ordination as a minister of the Word. From then on he wrote V.D.M. (*Verbi Divini Minister*, or Minister of the Word) behind his name.

It is not known whether his family attended his ordination. Part of the joy was tempered by the sorrow of the death of his father, Johannes, who had passed away that January. In spite of their religious differences, the family had remained on speaking terms. Father Johannes had even used his tinsmithing skills to fashion a portable nightlight for Vander Werp to use when traveling during evening hours.

Besides the protocol of the pulpit, there was the protocol of the *ambtsgewaad* or clerical attire. Many heated discussions were held concerning the correctness of wearing the standard costume, consisting of a long black coat, *kuitbroek* or knickers, and shirt with *befje*, a kind of bib consisting of two tabs said to represent the two tables of the law. It had been forgotten that this was essentially the costume of the well-to-do Dutch burgher of the eighteenth century; over time it had come to represent the garb especially reserved for clergy. Scholte preferred to wear the normal style of the day. The 1840 Synod of Amsterdam, in dealing with this question, decided that clergy should wear modest and fitting clothing that would not give offense. Although the synod did not make it mandatory, it recommended that ministers appear in the pulpit wearing the official clerical attire. Vander Werp chose to wear the

---

[14]   Wesseling, *Friesland*, 2: 243. Those who passed with Vander Werp were F. Redeker, Helenius de Cock, D. D. Drukker from Groningen, and Y. J. Veenstra, J. T. Bijzitter, H. Wiersma, and Sietze Baron from Friesland. H. de Vries and H. Vander Schuur of Groningen, and A. K. Vander Meer and Martin Ypma from Friesland were told to study some more. Martin Ypma, of Minnertsga, later served as pastor in Vriesland, Michigan.

Typical clerical attire in
the Netherlands

prescribed outfit. In this, he took his cues from his mentor, De Cock, who had wholeheartedly supported its use.[15]

His official ordination, plus the outward accoutrements—pulpit and clergy costume—signifying his status as a full member of the clergy, may also have given Vander Werp more assurance in his preaching. After this time, while he is commended for his preaching, there are no more references to the emotional rhetoric that characterized his preaching while *oefenaar*.

Spiritually, the seven years Vander Werp labored in Leeuwarden were blessed. Sunday services were well attended, so that within half a year the congregation had doubled and the building has been enlarged.[16] No doubt his preaching drew many, but church attendance may have increased because these were difficult years for the country, including Leeuwarden.

[15] De Cock, *De Cock*, 556-57. See also H. Beets, *De Chr. Geref. Kerk in Noord Amerika* (Grand Rapids: Grand Rapids Printing, 1918), 39.

[16] From the period August 1843 to April 1844, forty-four people made profession of faith and thirty other members were added.

The winter of 1844–45 was especially brutal.[17] For eighteen weeks ships lay frozen in the waterways, cutting off vital supply lines. Without means to pay for adequate heating fuel, many of the poor and elderly froze in their homes. Food prices soared. By June hunger riots broke out and mobs broke into the city's bakeries and grocery stores until the military restored order. The number of people on welfare rose to fifteen percent of the population. Vander Werp's own health suffered. Christmas fell on a Wednesday that year, which meant three extra services—two on Christmas Day, and one on the day after. Mercifully, his church council let him decide for himself whether he was physically able to preach the three extra sermons required during that Christmas week.[18]

The following summer brought the onset of the potato rot; the crops of 1846 and 1847 failed and food prices soared even higher. While the poor suffered, some looked to America as an answer. The departures of Van Raalte in October 1846 and Scholte in April 1847 with many followers did not go unnoticed in Friesland. A good number from this province also left.

On a wickedly cold winter day early in 1847, Jan Hendrik Vander Werp skated over the frozen waterways from his home in Bierum, province of Groningen, to the parsonage on Wisserstraat to announce that he too was leaving for America.

Jan Hendrik had been struggling financially for years. The severe winter of 1844-1845 ground all shipping to a virtual halt. Trapped in ice, his boat along with many others lay idle for weeks in the harbor. There were no government aid agencies to which he could turn. Nor could he turn to the church. One of the stipulations of the government had been that the new denomination take care of its own poor. However, there were so many poor by this time that the church could not provide adequate assistance to them.[19]

Jan Hendrik told his brother about his travel plans. He and his family were teaming up with the Werkman family and planned to

---

[17] Buisman, *Bar,* 208.
[18] At this time the Netherlands observed a Second Christmas Day with a morning service besides the two services on Christmas Day.
[19] J. van Gelderen. "Scheuring en Vereniging - 1827-1869" *De Afscheiding van 1834 en haar geschiedenis.* W. Bakker, et al. eds. (Kampen: Kok, 1984), 140-41. Even when the Dutch national constitution was rewritten in 1848, it kept the existing rule that municipalities and churches should look after their own poor and not look to the state for any assistance.

settle in Milwaukee.[20] Without mentioning it, both men knew why Jan Hendrik was not joining Van Raalte's group. They still blamed Van Raalte for taking De Cock away from their *Kruisgezinden* church, leaving them without a pastor for years. Van Raalte's more lenient interpretation of the Church Order did not sit well with them either. But more importantly, Van Raalte had sided with his brother-in-law, Simon Van Velzen, in vigorously opposing ordination for lay preachers. At the provincial gathering in Leeuwarden of January 3, 1843, he, along with Van Velzen, had denounced lay preaching as being against the scriptures, stating that it caused division in and damage to the church.[21]

If the idea of going to America crossed Vander Werp's mind at that time, he did not pursue it. The *Afgescheiden* churches in the Netherlands demanded a great deal of his time and energy. Traveling in Friesland and surrounding provinces on church-related matters also began exacting their toll on his health. He could not imagine how he had trekked around the country as much as he had in his younger days. Still, he did not try to hold Jan Hendrik back, but rather urged him to write about his journey and adventures.

Vander Werp had news to write as well. Three families from his congregation left for America in 1847.[22] In that same year he wrote about the cholera epidemic that caused many deaths in Leeuwarden. He also related the good news to Jan Hendrik—in particular how his family was growing. During these turbulent years, Albertje presented Vander Werp with three children: Reinder, born in 1847; Jan, born in 1848; and Catharine, born in 1850. But life was precarious and death a constant presence.

In the summer of 1849 Leeuwarden once again experienced a cholera epidemic resulting in numerous deaths. Vander Werp's younger

---

[20] Henry S. Lucas, *Dutch Immigrant Memoirs and Related Writings* (Grand Rapids: Eerdmans, 1997), 136-37.

[21] Wesseling, *Groningerland*, 3: 268. See also H. Algra, *Wonder*, 102-3. Bouwman, *Crisis*, 54, 58. Van Raalte and Brummelkamp often attended provincial gatherings as advising delegates, but Van Raalte walked out of the Frisian Provincial gathering of March 20, 1844, at which Vander Werp was examined and admitted to the ministry. Due to a conflict, Classis Leeuwarden had not been allowed to be seated at this provincial gathering and Van Raalte subsequently called the gathering illegitimate.

[22] Robert P. Swierenga, *Family Tree Maker's Family Archives, Immigration Records: Dutch in America, 1800s*, CD #269. Broderbund, 2000. Hendrik Brouwer, plumber, thirty-eight, wife and five children; Eelke DeJong, baker, forty, single; Abel Spanma, baker, forty, wife and three children.

brother, Hendrik, succumbed to the cholera raging in Groningen.[23] A year later, on June 10, 1850, his mother passed away and in March, 1851, Douwe and Albertje stood at the grave of their little four-year-old son, Reinder.

The dire economic circumstances drove the churches in the provinces to seek the Lord's mercy. At their provincial meeting held March 20 and 21, 1846, in Leeuwarden, those present requested the king to call a special national day of prayer for crops that same spring, to be followed by a thanksgiving service in the fall. Vander Werp and two other members signed this request.

In spite of, or perhaps because of, the general unrest among the people, Vander Werp initiated a rigorous church discipline program in Leeuwarden. Along with an elder he visited each family before serving Communion. This is not so surprising, if one takes into consideration that, according to the Seceders, one of the three marks of a true church is the administration of discipline.[24]

Among those attending his church in Leeuwarden was a young woman named Gerritdina Ten Brummelaar. Moved by his preaching, she struggled with her own doubts about belonging to God's elect—an inner battle she waged for three years. Vander Werp could not have foreseen then that this young woman would play a large part later in his life.

After seven years of harmonious rapport between pastor and consistory, the relationship became strained to the point where church visitors reported on the matter. Though the consistory members could find no fault with the pastor or his wife, they believed that when he received a call from Ferwerd, they could not in good conscience ask him to stay in Leeuwarden. Part of the problem seems to have been declining finances. Even though the pews were always occupied on Sundays, and pew rental income steady, finances were declining so that by the fall of 1851, the koster, or caretaker, had to be let go.[25]

Feeling that he could no longer work effectively under such strained circumstances, Vander Werp accepted a call to Ferwerd and moved his family out of the city into rural Friesland.

[23]   Hendrik, only thirty, was followed in death shortly after by his wife, leaving their children orphaned. One of those, Hendrik (1846-1918), also immigrated to the U.S.A., where he became a CRC minister and editor of the Banner.
[24]   The first two being the preaching of the Word and administration of the sacraments.
[25]   Wesseling, Friesland, 1: 246-47.

CHAPTER 11

Ferwerd and Lioessens

Located near the north coast of Friesland, Ferwerd sits elevated on a *terp* (prehistoric mound) overlooking the rich clay ground that is home to many imposing dairy farms. The 1849 census of Ferwerd listed 191 people as *Afgescheiden* and 1,416 as belonging to the Reformed Church, showing that twelve percent of the town's people had seceded. (The provincial average was just under two percent).[1] By 1851 the *Afgescheiden* congregation cited 450 members, a considerable growth; however, many of these may also have come from the surrounding countryside and nearby villages.[2]

If Vander Werp thought he was leaving the sins of the city behind, he was in for a surprise. His arrival in Ferwerd coincided with a catastrophe that touched the lives of almost all Frisian farmers, and that led to a considerable scandal in Ferwerd. The province had been in the grip of a highly contagious cattle disease, which in 1851 felled nearly six thousand cows. The carcasses of these animals were, as was normal and legal in those days, buried on the farmer's own land, or in open land along the roads and around the villages. It was illegal, however, to dig up these carcasses for any reason. About a decade earlier, the English had found that ground cattle bone made fine fertilizer and paid good money for these bones—a real temptation to rich and poor alike. In a sweep of the villages in the municipality of Ferwerderadeel by the

[1] L. H. Mulder, *Revolte der Fijnen: De Afscheiding van 1834 als sociaal conflict en sociale beweging* (Meppel: Boom, 1973), 386, 390.
[2] Organized by De Cock in 1835. The census numbers are from Mulder, *Revolte*, 377.

authorities in February and March 1852, 140 people were caught and sentenced with jail terms for exhuming cattle and selling their bones. It is not known if any of the offenders belonged to Vander Werp's congregation, but in a small village such as Ferwerd, where families are usually interrelated, this scandal touched nearly everyone.[3]

Another problem plaguing the population during most of the nineteenth century was alcoholism. D. Van Dijk, who grew up in the parsonage in Blija, Ferwerd's neighboring town, states that around 1834,

> Government statistics reported that every man, woman, and child consumed twelve bottles of hard liquor per year, not counting beer and wine. There were in that small town, four bars and a liquor store. Drink was served at any and all occasions.[4]

Thomas Hood, an English tourist in Holland in 1840, remarked that even little boys drank.

"To the Dutch," he wrote, "water was for washing and for sailing, but not for drinking."[5]

In a congress on poverty held in Groningen in 1854, alcoholism led the list of causes of poverty, followed directly by hasty and unwise marriages, poor money management, and unemployment. When someone at the meeting suggested that low wages might also be a contributing factor, he was told that "poverty is from God, and hunger should lead to hard work."[6] The Seceders may have preached against alcohol abuse, but they were not against its use. Drinking cut across all tiers of society—rich and poor—but the poor could least afford it. Nevertheless, for the poorer people, coffee and tea were not as affordable

---

[3]   D. R. Wildeboer, "Gevangenisstraf in 1852 voor beenderendelvers uit Hallum, Ferwerd, Marrum, Blija en Holwerd," *De Sneuper,* 49 (March 1999): 26-30.

[4]   D. Van Dijk, *Hoe het was, en hoe het geworden is* (Goes: Oosterbaan & Le Contre, 1960), 18.

[5]   Mathijsen, *Gemaskerde Eeuw*, 193. The situation had gotten so bad that the Society for the Common Good tried unsuccessfully to pass an anti-drinking law in 1838. The government believed that drinking could not be legislated and the church considered wine and liquor as gifts of God. Not until 1881 did the government pass a law curtailing drinking and prohibiting sales to minors. See also Melis te Velde, *Anthony Brummelkamp (1811-1888)* (Barneveld: De Vuurbaak, 1988), 452-3. Anthony Brummelkamp warned repeatedly against the evils of alcohol in *De Bazuin*.

[6]   Maarten Valken, ed., *Kroniek van Nederland* (Amsterdam: Elsevier Boeken, 1988), 711. See also Van Weerden, *Spanningen*, 299-304.

as cheap beer. Not until the Dutch invented a cheap brew from chicory root could the average man afford coffee made of chicory.

During the mid-nineteenth century, the chicory plant was Ferwerderadeel's main crop. The seed was sown in late April or early May, after which the plants were thinned out. The roots, harvested in October, were washed, chopped, dried, and roasted. Before the age of industrialization, harvesting these roots by hand was difficult and dirty work, especially during cold and rainy conditions. Many members of Vander Werp's congregation and their children worked in these chicory fields. When Vander Werp came to Ferwerd, the congregation was made up of only three fairly well-to-do farmers, a dozen market gardeners, approximately twenty small independent business people, such as a baker, shoemaker, and seamstress, and the remainder laborers—women as well as men.[7]

This congregation too benefited greatly from Vander Werp's ministry. Besides the regular catechism lessons, he initiated private lessons for the older members and those unable to read. Many poorer members had received limited or no schooling due to their family's economic circumstances, or had been kept out of school for religious reasons.[8] He preached three times a Sunday, and again on Thursday evenings. His installation text, Psalm 32:8, "I will instruct you and teach you the way you should go," revealed the enduring teacher in him.[9]

Another side of Vander Werp surfaced during the spring of 1853. When a nationwide uproar over the restoration of the Roman Catholic hierarchy in the Netherlands reached as far north as Ferwerd, Vander Werp sprang into action. Ever since the Dutch had driven the Spanish out of the Netherlands and the Reformation had gained the upper hand, Roman Catholics had not been allowed their own bishoprics in the United Provinces. Many Protestants considered the Pope the Antichrist and the Mass idolatry. When the Seceders strove for freedom to worship, they did not envision that the new constitution, written in 1848 and guaranteeing them religious liberty, would grant the same to Roman Catholics.[10] In April 1853, King William II officially welcomed

---

7   Mulder, *Revolte*, 392.
8   See chapter 8.
9   Wesseling, *Friesland*, 1:128.
10 Mulder, *Revolte*, 277. In 1829 population registers began on a national basis. In the 1849 census a category for *Afgescheiden* was added. The population of Friesland as of Nov. 19, 1849, was 247,360, of which 205,670 were Protestant (4,698 of those were *Afgescheiden*), 20,017 Roman Catholic, 1,945 Jews, and the remainder specified no religious affiliation.

Archbishop Johannes Zwijsen (1794-1877) to the Netherlands. When Pope Pius IX established five new dioceses in1853 (Utrecht, Haarlem, Breda,'s-Hertogenbosch, and Roermond), Protestants protested to such an extent that the government of Prime Minister Johan Thorbecke collapsed. Vander Werp gathered more than ninety signatures personally, adding them to the 200,000 gathered nationwide on a petition presented to the king urging him to retract this decision. Besides the signatures, many brochures and articles expressed their outrage in what came to be called the April *Beweging* (Initiative). By involving himself in this issue, Vander Werp adhered to De Cock's teaching regarding the Roman Catholic Church. In 1840, the year Vander Werp studied with De Cock, the latter had written a scathing denouncement of the Roman Catholic Church, entitled *Het Beest en de Roomsche Afgoderij (The Beast and Roman Catholic Idolatry).*[11]

Fearing civil war, a new government hastily enacted a law forbidding all Roman Catholic priests to wear their priestly garments in public, hoping that this would appease the Protestants and put a damper on Catholic processions and so avert unrest. Religion, they argued, was a private matter, and therefore all outward appearances of it should be confined to the sanctuary. Of course the same law applied to other denominations as well, and from then on Vander Werp could wear his clerical attire only on Sundays in the pulpit, no longer during the week in public.[12]

His involvement in the action against Roman Catholics and their freedom to worship showed a less gracious side of Vander Werp. He demanded freedom to worship for the Seceders, yet seemed unwilling to extend that same privilege to others.

As in his other congregations, so also in Ferwerd, he recorded personally all the council minutes, and in the minutes of June 26, 1854, he reported with great joy that the General Synod of 1854 held in Zwolle, to which he had been a delegate, had decided to establish a theological school in Kampen, in the province of Overijssel. The same synod had invited each province to elect one of its own pastors to

---

[11]   H. De Cock, *Het Beest en de Roomsche Afgoderij verdedigd weer op nieuw; doch op nieuw ook weersproken en wederlegd naar Gods Woord* (n. p. 1840).

[12]   M. J. Aalders, "Het ambtsgewaad ter discussie in de kring der afgescheiden," *Predikant in Nederland (1800 tot heden) Jaarboek voor de geschiedenis van het Nederlands Protestantisme na 1800,* D. Th. *Kuiper,* et. al. eds. Vol. 5, (Kampen: Kok, n.d.), 155.

become a trustee of the new school, and at the first provincial gathering Vander Werp was chosen as the trustee for Friesland.[13]

When in due time he received two calls, the Ferwerd church tried to keep him by offering him a one-hundred-guilder annual increase in salary. He declined the calls; however, shortly after he accepted a call to Lioessens. Although the congregation had seemed happy to keep him, a number of the council members voiced some criticism when preparing his membership papers to be sent on. *Dominee*, they complained, had been unable to complete all the family visits for the year and had visited the home of one prominent member too much. Vander Werp defended

---

The Kampen Theological School

Twenty years after the *Afscheiding* in Ulrum, during which time ordained pastors chosen for the task gave theological instruction, a theological school was officially opened December 6, 1854 in Kampen, Province of Overijssel. The first professors were Anthony Brummelkamp, Helenius De Cock (son of Hendrik De Cock), Tamme De Haan, and Simon Van Velzen. The first curators (board of trustees) were B. De Beij, representative for the Province of Groningen; D. J. Vander Werp representative for the Province of Friesland; and W. A. Kok, representative for the Province of Drenthe. Vander Werp served as clerk for the year 1855. There were thirty-seven students present at the opening. The idea of a theological school had long been a dream of the Seceders. At the Synod of 1846 in Groningen, the matter had been discussed, but tabled, and instead the Reverend Tamme De Haan was chosen as the instructor for the provinces of Groningen and Friesland. It was brought up again at the Synod of 1849 in Amsterdam, and Franeker, in the Province of Friesland, was suggested as a possible location, but no final decision was made. Not until the Synod of 1854 in Zwolle was the matter decided and Kampen chosen as the city. Vander Werp's term as Friesland's representative ended in 1857 when he moved to North Holland, but he served another term as the representative from that province for the year 1860-1861 [J. van Gelderen and F. Rozemond, eds. *Gegevens betreffende de Theologische Universiteit Kampen 1854-1995* (Kampen: Kok, 1994)].

---

[13]   J. Van Gelderen and F. Rozemond, eds. *Gegevens betreffende de Theologische Universiteit Kampen 1854-1995* (Kampen: Kok, 1994).

himself by stating that in the summer it was difficult to find people at home because they were out working. In the winter he had to preach three to four times a week, while teaching six to seven catechism classes. There really was not much time left. Besides, he chided them, had he not fulfilled all the obligations for which they had called him? And now with his leaving, had he earned these accusations? Perhaps Vander Werp recalled the sour note that had marked his farewell in Leeuwarden, and he wanted these people to remember him as having done his best.[14]

The two calls Vander Werp had declined were from the flourishing cities of Bolsward, Friesland, and Winschoten, Groningen. Instead, he moved his family further up the northern coast of Friesland to the small village of Lioessens. Perhaps he accepted the call because he knew the people there from his days in Ulrum with De Cock and valued the steadfastness of their faith in spite of hardships.

Lioessens, Friesland, is on the same geographical latitude as Ulrum in Groningen, but until the 1900s, the two were separated by the Lauwerszee.[15] Still, the detour around this considerable body of water had not stopped some of the residents from walking to Ulrum in the 1830s. Stijntje Buwalda, a twenty-eight-year-old widow and shopkeeper, was the first one to walk the twenty-five kilometers to Ulrum to attend De Cock's services.[16] Later, when more joined her, they would pass the five-hour walking time by singing psalms.

The pastor of the Reformed church did not appreciate Stijntje's Sunday's activities, and soon after she began making her treks to Ulrum, she had to appear before the consistory. When she explained why she wanted to attend church in Ulrum and not in Lioessens, the minister and consistory withdrew her shop lease, forcing her out. They also made her and her two children walk through town singing psalms. "If you are so pious," they mocked her, "you should show it."

"That looks bad, but really isn't so, *dominee*," she is said to have answered, "because the God of Elijah still lives."[17] The *dominee* harassing Stijntje was Jodokus Reddingius, of the same Reddingius clergy dynasty as Benthem-Reddingius from Assen, who had given De Cock in Ulrum

---

14 Wesseling, *Friesland*, 1, 130.
15 Now called Lauwersmeer.
16 Widow of Arjen Kornelis Ludema; she later married Jan Reiding.
17 "Dat liket slim, mar is net sa slim, dymnij, hwant de God fan Elia libbet noch."
18 T. A. Romein, *Naamlijst der Predikanten sedert de Hervorming tot nu toe in de Hervormde Gemeenten van Friesland* (Leeuwarden: A Meijer, et al, 1888), 562, 707. In Friesland alone seventeen members of this family served the Reformed Church during the seventeen and eighteen hundreds. J. H. Reddingius served the Reformed Church of Lioessens from 1842-1883, which included the years that Vander Werp served in Lioessens. Given Reddingius's treatment of the Seceders in his town, there was probably not much of a collegial relationship between the two.

Students, trustees, and professors of the newly founded Kampen Theological School, 1854. Vander Werp is second from left in the front row.

and Vander Werp in Smilde their share of grief.[18]

The little group of Seceders in Lioessens had formed a congregation in 1851, and in November 1854 Vander Werp became its first pastor. The fact that it took the Lioessen church three years to acquire a pastor was due in part to the ratio of Seceder congregations to pastors. The thirty-four *Afgescheiden* congregations that had formally organized since 1834 had only twenty-three pastors to serve them. It may also have been due to the church's inability to support a minister financially. There were not many well-to-do among their numbers, but with sacrificial giving, they were able to raise an annual salary of three hundred and sixty-one guilders for Vander Werp.[19] This amount was less than half of the eight hundred guilders he had received in Leeuwarden, but, unlike Leeuwarden, Lioessens provided a parsonage.

Vanderwerp and Albertje and their children, Jan, Catharine, and Reinder arrived at their new home a few days before his installation service. [20] In Lioessens, as in Leeuwarden, Vander Werp organized

[19] A. Algra, *De historie gaat door het eigen dorp* (Leeuwarden: Friesch Dagblad, 1956), 5: 267.
[20] This Reinder was named after the Reinder who passed away in Leeuwarden. The children's ages were Jan, six; Catharine, four; and Reinder, one. His oldest son, Johannes, son of his first wife born in 1836 was eighteen years old at this time and not listed with the children arriving in Lioessens. He may have already joined the military since at the time of his death in 1864 he was a career military man.

regular house visitations and a mid-week service on Thursdays at five p.m. if the moon was out. But only three months into getting to know this congregation, grief struck again when on February 24, 1855, Albertje passed away. At age thirty-seven, Albertje had not quite reached the average life span of thirty-eight years for women at the time. Sad as it was, it was not totally unexpected in an age when death hovered relentlessly. Almost daily one was reminded of death's prominence and presence by the tolling of the church bells, the customary wearing of black clothes by mourners for a year, and the frequent funeral processions in full view of all.[21]

But knowledge of statistical averages does not lessen grief. With no one to oversee the busy household and the three young children, Albertje's death was a heavy loss for Vander Werp, whose whole life was taken up with work in his own church and in the denomination at large. Yet in spite of his family's situation, he became correspondent, or clerk, for Classis Dokkum during this time, and along with Jan R. Kreulen from Hallum and Klaas J. Pieters from Franeker, he worked on a publication defending the Secession.[22]

The three wrote the booklet titled, *Apology: Is the Secession in the Netherlands from the Dutch Reformed Church from God or from People?* to answer the criticism of the Seceders.[23] By 1854, two decades after De Cock's secession, the government-instigated persecution had ended, but the Seceders were far from being accepted.[24] They were seen as antisocial and fanatical in their observance of the letter of the law, and they were often accused of polarizing families and villages, even by conservative members of the Reformed Church.

---

[21] Mathijsen, *Gemaskerde Eeuw*, 108. "Vrouwen werden in 1840 gemiddeld nog niet ouder dan achtendertig jaar, mannen nog geen zesendertig. Van elke vier kinderen die geboren werden, stierf er een voor zijn eerste levensjaar, en van de overgeblevenden stierf nog een kwart voor het zesde jaar." ["In 1840 the average age of women was no more than thirty-eight years; men did not make thirty-six. Of every four children born, one died before the age of one, and one-quarter of the remaining died before their sixth birthday."]

[22] H. J. Pieters, D. J. Vander Werp, and J. H. Kreulen, *Apologie: Is de Afscheiding in Nederland van het Hervormd Kerkgenootschap uit God of uit de Menschen?* (Franeker: T. Telenga), 1856.

[23] Ibid.

[24] L. Penning, *Uit mijn leven* (Zwolle: La Riviere & Voorhoeve, 1927), 9-24. In this autobiography, best selling Dutch author Lourence Penning described the persecution his family suffered while living in the parsonage in Waardhuizen, Noord Brabant, where his father was an *Afgescheiden* pastor from 1851-1861.

One of the critics was the Reformed minister, J. W. Felix of Heeg, Province of Friesland, who wrote an article in the *Friese Kerkelijk Maandblad* (*Frisian Church Monthly*), in which he attacked the Seceders. This accusation was answered by J. Talsma from Donkerbroek in an article in *De Bazuin* (*Trumpet*—the official organ of the *Afgescheiden*, edited by the Reverend Anthony Brummelkamp and originating in Kampen), which was again answered by Felix in a series of articles comparing the Seceders to the Baptists and other splinter groups such as the Free Evangelicals, *Ledeboergezinden* (followers of L. C. G. Ledeboer, a minister who professed not to study before writing a sermon, but to preach as it was given to him by the Holy Spirit), Anabaptists, and others.[25] Because Felix painted the Seceders with the same brush as those other groups, Vander Werp, Pieters, and Kreulen felt the need to defend the Secession even twenty years after the fact.[26]

Due to his exceptional talent for organization and his tenacity, Vander Werp had gained a reputation as a leader, preacher, and teacher in the Secessionist movement. Nevertheless, he also needed to learn from others, in particular from his colleague, Kreulen, who unlike himself had received a formal classical education.

In Hallum, as in many other villages, there were groups of believers who sympathized with the Seceders, but did not want to break their ties with the Reformed Church. These people formed separate worship groups and would sometimes attend the Secessionists' services, only to hear the minister preach sermons urging them to leave their own churches. This aggressive preaching often caused bad blood in families, and Kreulen was of the opinion not to force the issue; he felt one should only preach the gospel and let the Word of God convict people. This caring and nurturing man may have influenced the more confrontational Vander Werp for the good. Thus in their *Apologia* they promoted preaching God's Word and discouraged ranting and raving against those who had not joined the Secession. In small villages where families were divided, the healing words of pastors like Kreulen did much to salve wounds.

Pieters, Vander Werp's friend from Franeker, also helped him in a very personal way. After Albertje's death, he recommended his sister-in-law, Hendrikje Karsten, as a housekeeper. Sometime during that spring

---

[25] J. Bosch, *Figuren en Aspecten uit de Eeuw der Afscheiding* (Goes: Oosterbaan & Le Cointre NV, 1952), 179.

[26] See chapter 19 for more about this *Apologie*.

Meppel

or summer, the thirty-six-year-old grocer's daughter traveled from
Meppel in the province of Drenthe to Friesland, to take up her duties
as a live-in housekeeper. It seems that Vander Werp and Hendrikje got
along well, for on June 20, 1856, they were married in Meppel. Pieters
served as a witness at the wedding. A year later, in May 1857, Vander
Werp accepted a call to Broek op Langedijk in the province of North
Holland. And as usual when he moved, he hired a *beurtschipper*, loaded
his family and material goods on board, and set off for a new challenge
in an entirely different part of the country.

CHAPTER 12

North Holland and Gerritdina

Vander Werp, Hendrikje, and the children arrived in Broek op Langedijk in the Province of North Holland in early March 1857. A gardening community, Broek op Langedijk supplied fresh vegetables to the markets of the cities farther south.[1] Here Vander Werp not only had to adjust to a new congregation but also to new regional customs. Unlike the people in Friesland, Groningen, and Drenthe, the people in the northern part of the Province of North Holland had not been close to the events in Ulrum. Compared to the Province of Groningen, which had no less than 12,116 *Afgescheiden* in 1857, there were only 3,093 in the more populated Province of North Holland.[2] Even after they were organized as a congregation, the congregation of Broek op Langedijk associated with the *Kruisgezinden* until 1847, consequently many were strangers to Vander Werp.

One month later, in April 1857, Vander Werp received a letter from his brother, Jan Hendrik, informing him of another secession—this time in America.[3] A group had formally split away from the established

---

[1] While the Dutch word "broek" in most cases means "trousers," in geographical terminology it means "poldered in" land, or marshland.

[2] Beets, *De Chr. Geref. Kerk*, 35.

[3] Although an actual letter does not exist, we may assume the brothers corresponded, according to Henry Vander Werp, *An Outline of the History of the Christian Reformed Church of America* (Holland, Mich.: H. Holkeboer, 1898), 39. Henry Vander Werp, Douwe's nephew, cites private correspondence as a source of information about what was happening in the church in the United States. See also John A. Westervelt,

Broek of Langedijk harbor

Reformed Church in America, calling itself the Holland Reformed Church. Although later in his life this action so far away would have great consequences for him, at the moment Vander Werp had more than enough to think about concerning his new congregation. Still, the choice of name was not lost on him. The *Kruisgezinden* had always insisted on keeping the word *Gereformeerd*, Reformed, as part of their name, and Jan Hendrik may have had a say in the matter. The others would certainly have agreed with him.

At home, the children had to get used to their new stepmother and new schools. This difficult time of adjustment for the family turned even more tragic when, after only two years of marriage, Hendrikje passed away June 25, 1858. Again Vander Werp was left with his four children: Johannes, a young man of twenty-two; Jan, ten; Catherine, eight; and Reinder, five years old. We do not know how he managed to do his work and look after his children at the same time. In all likelihood he hired a maid for the household chores; the women of the congregation may also have helped out. His only sister, Grietje, was a married woman with a family of her own.[4] She may have been able to

---

"Rev. D. J. Vander Werp," *Banner of Truth*, 39/10 (May 6, 1904): 147-48, "This was made manifest by letters written to his parents, brothers and sisters."

[4]   Grietje Vander Werp married Lui Bottema in 1850. Their two daughters, Aafjen and Catharine were born in 1852 and 1854, respectively.

take in one of the children for some time, but not look after the family. Vander Werp stayed in Broek op Langedijk only two years and then moved the family to Den Helder in March 1859.

Being a single pastor with children presented a problem. With a salary barely sufficient to keep himself and his family going, he could ill afford to hire a full-time housekeeper. Also, as a pastor he had to keep up an impeccable moral appearance, something not easily done with a single woman in his home day and night. Therefore, finding another wife became an urgent matter for him; he had no time to pursue and court a woman leisurely. Pondering his options, he remembered the young woman in his Leeuwarden congregation—the one who had so earnestly searched for and found the Lord. She met all the criteria for a pastor's wife—a devout Christian, a hard worker, someone who knew social graces, having worked in a well-to-do-home, and who had experience looking after children. He asked for her hand in marriage early in the spring of 1859.

Gerritdina Ten Brummelaar, a serious young woman of almost thirty, had, like so many others at the time, experienced all the soul-wrenching emotions of conversion and of leaving the state church to join the Secession. Reading through her journal, one senses that even accepting Vander Werp's marriage proposal was for her not so much a romantic decision as a spiritual one.

Gerritdina's ancestors came from the province of Overijssel, the Netherlands. On April 15, 1824, her parents, Derk Ten Brummelaar and Willemina Vierdag were married in Zwolle and by 1828 had moved to Kampen, where Derk operated a hostelry and also earned his keep as a traveling salesman.[5] In 1830, the year of Gerritdina's birth, the city of Kampen had not yet gained status as the seat of the theological school of the *Afgescheiden,* as it would in later years. Once an important Hanseatic League city, Kampen had declined to a sleepy, picturesque port by the 1800s.

As the third child in a family of nine children, Gerritdina knew from a young age what it was like to look after little children, help around the house, and meet the public who stayed at their inn. Fortunately, her education was not neglected. Letters written later in life reflect a beautiful penmanship and intelligent expression of thought. Her family belonged to the Reformed Church, and the Secession had not swayed them from their conviction that the Secessionists were mostly

[5]   The name Ten Brummelaar was changed to Brummeler in America.

Koornmarkt
gate in
Kampen

uneducated religious fanatics. They may have based their bias on the
fact that in Kampen the Seceders did not have a good reputation. In
a report about the membership of the Secessionist Church in the
Netherlands, dated April 1, 1836, the members of the congregation in
Kampen were described as "nearly all from the lower socioeconomic
class, and many not well mannered." On Sunday, February 14, after the
windows of their clandestine meeting house had been smashed in, the
resulting melee had to be put down with military intervention.[6] This
did not mean that the Ten Brummelaars themselves were lacking in
faith or were not good church people, because according to Gerritdina,
"We had a good moral and virtuous upbringing." She responded to that

---

[6]   F. L. Bos, ed., *Archiefstukken betreffende de Afscheiding van 1834*, 4 vols. (Kampen: J. H.
       Kok, 1939-1946), 3, 175.

upbringing by making profession of faith in the Reformed Church at age eighteen.[7]

Shortly after that Gerritdina's life took a dramatic turn when, like so many adult girls of her class, she took a position as a maidservant. The fact that Gerritdina was already eighteen before she worked outside the home meant that either she was needed at home or her family was sufficiently well off for her not to have to find work at fourteen or sixteen years of age, as many of the poorer girls were destined to do.

For the next decade she worked for the well-to-do P. D. Simon family in Leeuwarden. She journeyed from Kampen to Leeuwarden by boat across the Zuiderzee to Lemmer in Friesland, and from Lemmer to Leeuwarden by canal boat. This was not a difficult journey, but not one she would make every weekend, because maids in those days were given very little personal time off, one Sunday a month at the most. Whatever communication she had with her family during those years was done by letter.

Being a domestic in the Netherlands in the 1800s meant a life of hard work from sunup to sundown. Without laborsaving appliances, a maid's work began early in the day laying the fires and preparing breakfast. After that she scrubbed floors, washed and ironed clothes, did the marketing, tended the children and completed a hundred other tasks which were a normal part of everyday life. In a short memoir written later in life, Gerritdina mentioned how she rinsed clothes in the water of the canal by hanging over the side of a small rowboat. Still, the hard physical life paled in comparison to the efforts she expended on behalf of her soul.

Once in Leeuwarden, a worldly city by all accounts, Gerritdina determined to live a "moral and virtuous life." In all likelihood her parents, as parents are wont to do, before she left home lectured her to "behave herself."[8] Her employer may also have pointed out the pitfalls of living in a city such as Leeuwarden, with its many temptations. But she had not been informed that in spite of her "morality and virtuosity," she stood in grave danger of losing her soul unless she had a conversion experience. This news she received from Leentje Veluwenkamp, the Simon family's other maid, who belonged to the Secessionists. Leentje soon witnessed to Gerritdina and admonished her that she would

---

[7]   Vander Werp-Lokker Collection, Calvin College Archives.

[8]   Helen J. Martz, *The Family of Dirk J. Ten Brummelaar, 1804-1864* (Evanston, Ill.: Privately printed, 1981). In a letter written by Willemina Ten Brummelaar before leaving the Netherlands in 1864, she admonished her adult children how to live.

surely perish unless she became aware of her sinful state and the need for a Savior. At Leentje's invitation, Gerritdina accompanied her to the Secessionist church services and heard Vander Werp preach on the text, "Everyone therefore who acknowledges me before others, I will also acknowledge before my Father in heaven; but whoever denies me before others, I will also deny before my Father in heaven."[9] About that sermon, she wrote later, "I had never before heard a minister speak so directly to two kinds of people in his message, implying that the hearers were either saved or unsaved. This put me in the class of the unconverted or unsaved who would be lost forever."[10]

The ensuing struggle about her soul's salvation caused her much grief. In order to find peace and assurance, Gerritdina began to attend Vander Werp's services regularly, thereby neglecting her own. Her employers, however, as members of the Reformed Church, wanted her to continue going to their church. They told her she shouldn't take religious matters too seriously—that she was a fine person and would surely go to heaven. Her own family took a much harder line. In many stern letters they warned her to have nothing to do with the Seceders. They did not want their well-raised daughter to associate with them. Her parents may also have worried that the Simons might let her go. Many employers belonging to the Reformed Church dismissed their hired men and maids when the latter joined Secessionist churches. They went to great lengths ordering her to attend the Reformed Church, even sending elders from their church to visit her on two occasions—but to no avail. Gerritdina's struggle continued for nearly three and a half years. Her struggle was not whether she would associate with the Seceders against her parents' will, but rather whether she herself was saved.

During this time she would often visit the Vander Werps to unburden her soul. Even when the Vander Werp family moved to Ferwerd, she continued writing to them. Still, in spite of her prayers and searching the scriptures, the assurance that she was saved eluded her. At one point she truly believed she belonged to the "unsaved" and became so depressed she could hardly eat or drink. She dared not even go to sleep.

As her despair about her lost state deepened, those around her hardly knew how to deal with her. Leentje would not let her go into the

---

[9]   Matthew 10: 32, 33, NRSV.
[10] Vander Werp-Lokker Collection, Calvin College Archives.

Gerritdina

boat alone to rinse out the laundry for fear she would do something foolish. Then, on June 30, 1851, at midday when she had reached a moment of total hopelessness, she prayed aloud, "Lord, I know I deserve to be eternally cast out of thy presence. My sins rise up against me. Is there no hope for such a one as I?" And then the words of Jeremiah 31:3 resounded in her ears. "I have loved you with an everlasting love; therefore I have continued my faithfulness to you." It was the turning point in her faith crisis. From then on she could accept that Jesus had died for her as well. Once fully assured, she immediately shared the good news with Leentje, and the two rejoiced together.[11]

The Secessionists strove for purity of living. For people such as Gerritdina, who already lived a virtuous life, that meant searching ever

[11]   Ibid.

deeper for ways to please God. Gerritdina chafed under the fact that her employers often entertained on Sundays, for this meant that she had to work on those days, not only doing the necessary but also frivolous tasks. Strict Sunday observance was for many common laborers and domestics almost impossible, as someone had to cook the meals, feed the family, and tend the cattle. She began to pray earnestly that the Lord would find a way out for her, so that she did not have to work so many Sundays. How the Lord would solve her problem she left entirely up to him. The answer came from a most unexpected source—a marriage proposal from *Dominee* Vander Werp, who recently had been widowed for the third time.

A domestic position like Gerritdina's offered little "career advancement." The most that one could hope for would be to become a "first" maid in a wealthy household, or a housekeeper in a home where the mistress had passed away. The housekeeper position afforded more status than a maid. She earned more and had more say in running the household. The other escape from her station in life was by the time-honored tradition of marriage, and starting one's own household.

In her memoirs, written later in her life, Gerritdina wrote,

> I felt that this was no doubt an answer to my prayer for deliverance from my Sunday work and other things that bothered me there. The Lord had said to me, "I have heard thy sighing and seen thy tears." Nevertheless, I could visualize many difficulties. *Dominee* Vander Werp was nineteen years older and a widower with three children [at home]. To take upon myself the great responsibilities involved was not a small matter. Also thinking of the duties of a minister's wife weighed heavily. After much prayer and coming to the conclusion that it was God's will that I should do so, I agreed and beseeched the Lord for his grace to carry out what was involved.[12]

The two were married May 27, 1859, in Den Helder, where Vander Werp had become the pastor only two months before. Looking back on the decision she made, Gerritdina wrote, "The Lord blessed us with love and peace. The three children loved me and I loved them. Later we had five more children."[13]

---

[12]   Ibid.
[13]   Ibid.

The devotion of the children to Gerritdina and the respect they accorded her during her life speak to the warm and loving qualities she brought to the marriage. Years later Vander Werp would write about her, "God blessed me with my fourth wife. She is a constant example to me in my Christian walk."[14]

Whatever her feelings for Vander Werp were at the time of their marriage, love grew over the years, as did Gerritdina's role as mother and pastor's wife. From her wedding day on, she would be respectfully referred to as "Juffrouw Vander Werp." The correct Dutch word for a married woman of some standing was "*mevrouw*" and "*juffrouw*" for a single woman. Yet, *juffrouw* became the designated title for the wives of Seceder pastors. Wives of Reformed pastors were referred to as "*mevrouw*." Because many Seceder pastors' wives, such as Gerritdina, came from the lower classes, society at large did not want to accord them the same status. The term "*juffrouw*" came to America with these women and lasted well into the next century.[15]

The couple lived in Den Helder for the first two years of their marriage. With Gerritdina taking over the care of the children and household duties, Vander Werp found time to use his exceptional organizational skills to gather all the synodical decisions of the Secession church to date in the Netherlands and publish them in 1859.[16]

While his family situation had stabilized, Vander Werp's time in Den Helder as pastor was stressful. The congregation of Den Helder had a difficult history. When it was founded under the leadership of Willem Wust, the congregation had joined the small *Kruisgezinden* denomination that had ordained Wust, a lay preacher, without the proper educational requirement that the Seceders insisted upon. When Wust left in 1846 because of some differences of opinion, the congregation called Wilhelmus van Leeuwen, who had also been ordained in the *Kruisgezinden* group according to Article 8 of the

14   Dirk Postma Collection, The Library of the Gereformeerde Kerk, Potchefstroom, Vander Werp to Postma, letter dated January 3, 1868, "God zegent mij met mijn vierde vrouw. Zij is mij veel tot een voorbeeld in leven voor den Heere."

15   Algra, *Wonder*, 243.

16   D. J. Vander Werp, ed. *Synodale besluiten der Christelijke Afgescheidene Gereformeerde Kerk in Nederland van 1836-1837: Bijeenverzameld en van een algemene register voorzien* (Kampen: Van Velzen Jr., 1859).

Dortian Church Order.[17] A schoolteacher prior to becoming a minister, he hoped to move up the ecclesiastical ladder by becoming a pastor in the larger Secessionist denomination. To achieve that goal, he pressed the Den Helder congregation to join the Secessionists' church, and in 1853 it became a member congregation. But the six years that followed were full of strife. An ongoing debate about building a church drained much time away from spiritual matters. Van Leeuwen had also pushed for a Christian school. Although Christian schools were allowed by this time, the entire cost had to be absorbed by the small congregation. The school only lasted a few years before it had to close due to bankruptcy. As almost always happens when large sums of money are involved, accusations and finger pointing added insult to injury. Early in the year 1861, after only two years in Den Helder, at the same consistory meeting at which the schoolteacher handed in his resignation, Vander Werp announced that he had accepted the call to Burum, Friesland.

[17] Article 8 of the Church Order of Dort; (more recently this has become Article 7 of the CRC Church Order): "a) Those who have not received the prescribed theological training but who give evidence that they are singularly gifted as to godliness, humility, spiritual discretion, wisdom, and the native ability to preach the Word, may, by way of exception, be admitted to the ministry of the Word, especially when the need is urgent. b) The classis, in the presence of the synodical deputies, shall examine these men concerning the required exceptional gifts. With the concurring advice of the synodical deputies, classis shall proceed as circumstances may warrant and in accordance with synodical regulations."

CHAPTER 13

Burum and Emigration

The *Schipsloot*, the waterway connecting Burum to the rest of the country, ended in a small harbor in the middle of the village. Here, in the spring of 1861, the *beurtschipper* hired by Vander Werp, now a mature fifty-year-old pastor, unloaded the family's household goods onto a wagon, to be delivered to the parsonage next to the *Christelijke Afgescheiden Kerk* on Herenstraat. Vander Werp had been called by the congregation of Burum to be its new pastor, and many of the older members of the congregation were no strangers to him. As he settled in and became reacquainted with the people, he must have reminisced with them about the events of 1835 and before, when many Burumers had made the long trek to Ulrum time and again over poor roads and in all kinds of weather to listen to De Cock preach, and how in 1835 De Cock had come to Burum to organize the congregation. The weather during the spring and summer months of that year had been warm and dry—a blessing not lost on the Seceders. Many had traveled from far and wide to gather in clandestine places, sometimes out in the open, to hear De Cock preach, baptize their children, and organize them into Secessionist congregations. Such had been the gathering held in Burum June 25, 1835.

People had come from many different villages and towns to one central place—the isolated farm of young Jan Paulus Ellens—situated in the countryside, far away from the prying eyes of the law. Ellens had set aside his fears of fines and arrest to offer his place for this very important gathering. By ten o'clock the barn was filled to overflowing.

Sipkesstraat in Burum

Due to a shortage of benches, many stood, while others, tired from their long walk, sat on the barn floor. The appointed *voorzanger* set the tone and soon their voices lifted up the old favorite Psalm 25:2 *"Heer, Ai maak mij Uwe wegen, door Uw Woord en Geest bekend."* ("Lord, make your way known to us according to your Word and Spirit.")

After the singing, De Cock opened the scriptures and preached on 2 Corinthians 6:17 and 18. Following the sermon, during a call for membership, thirty-nine people stepped forward and signed the charter of subscription, thereby instituting the first *Afgescheiden* congregation in Friesland.[1]

Two elders and two deacons were elected and installed. Then, after another sermon, De Cock baptized three children. At the end of the service, twenty-two-year-old Pieter Kornelis Radema was chosen to be the congregation's lay leader. By the time the authorities had gotten wind of the gathering and had dispatched messengers to Leeuwarden to ask for instructions as to how to penalize those present, the group had disbanded and escaped being fined.

When Vander Werp arrived twenty-six years later, the church had a parsonage and a proper church edifice. A recent need to add more seating had been solved by adding a balcony. The newly laid gravel road connecting Burum to the Friese Straatweg—a major brick

[1]   Burum Gereformeerde Kerk Minutes, June 21, 1835.

Entrance to Gereformeerde Kerk in Burum showing parsonage (*left*)
and consistory meeting building (*right*)

highway linking Leeuwarden with Groningen, the capital cities of the provinces of Friesland and Groningen—provided easier access to the markets of these cities. The bustling little town boasted 275 houses and a population of 1,650, of which approximately 1,100 were Reformed, 500 Seceders, several Mennonites, and two Roman Catholics. The geographical area making up the parish also included forty-five outlying farms. These thriving vegetable, grain, and dairy farms added to the general prosperity of the area. Because a number of these well-to-do farmers were Seceders, the congregation was able to look after its own poor.

As in his previous congregations, Vander Werp immediately organized a Thursday evening mid-week prayer service in Burum. Before 1890, when Abraham Kuyper organized the *Gereformeerde Kerken*, men's and women's societies, and young men's and young women's societies were unheard of, therefore mid-week teaching services were means used to spur growth and foster spirituality in the members.

Burum had a reputation as a sound and healthy congregation; there is no mention of disputes, arguments, or other internal strife in its consistory minutes. So sensitive, in fact, were the members to the financial straits of their less fortunate brothers and sisters, knowing the latter usually did not have any money when attending church, that

Hoogstraat in Burum

they did away with collections during the services. Those who could pay pledged their gifts, which were collected during the week. Vander Werp's predecessor, Frens Strik, stayed in Burum for fourteen and a half years—an indication that the congregation appreciated its pastors. For Vander Werp and Gerritdina, it may have seemed that the Lord in his wisdom had provided this place for some much needed peace and harmony in their lives. Later, when living in the United States and writing to friends in Burum, Gerritdina mentioned many other friends, indicating that in this Frisian village she and her husband were loved and accepted and among friends. Vander Werp may well have looked forward to a long and happy ministry in Burum, had he not received that life-changing call from America.

When, sometime in August 1863, Vander Werp received a call from the Christian Reformed Church in Graafschap, Michigan, to "come over and help us," he declined.[2] When, late in December of that same year, the call came a second time, he declined again.[3] He had good reasons to do so. He was well aware that the Graafschap congregation

---

[2]   Graafschap CRC Minutes, July 27, 1863. Article 3. Salary set at $400, free firewood, and free living in parsonage. The call letter was also dated July 27, 1863.

[3]   Ibid., Minutes December 9, 1863, Article 1.

Farm of Paulus Ellens near Burum where the first Seceder
congregation in Friesland was organized, June 25, 1835

belonged to a newly formed denomination that was not officially
recognized by his own denomination in the Netherlands. From the very
beginning in 1857, the members of the Christian Reformed Church had
applied to the Secessionist Church in the Netherlands to be part of its
fellowship. However, the Secessionist Church, not sure what the group
of emigrants thousands of miles away was all about, sent its regrets.
According to one author, "For Dutch pastors there was a deep suspicion
that the CRC was an ill-gotten child in search of legitimacy."[4]

Vander Werp knew first hand the struggles and conflicts of a few
leaders trying to hold together a diverse group of believers. He recalled
his association with the *Kruisgezinden* and remembered their unbending
spirit. Did he really want to embroil himself again in such controversy?
He knew the hardship, the pitfalls, the power struggles generated by
those wishing to start a new denomination. He had been there before.
As De Cock's right hand man, he had experienced all the pain and
difficulties of secession. His reluctance to throw himself into another
religious maelstrom is understandable. The reports coming from

[4]   James Schaap, *Our Family Album: The Unfinished Story of the Christian Reformed Church*
      (Grand Rapids: CRC Publications, 1998), 177.

The Schipsloot in Burum

America did not speak all that favorably about the spiritual situation of the brethren there either. In fact, one of his colleagues, Bernardus De Beij from Middelstum, Province of Groningen, called them "zealots without love and makers of sects."[5] Such was their reputation in the Netherlands.

Then there was the passage across the ocean to consider. Ship travel in 1864, though somewhat improved, was still a perilous business. Besides that, letters testified to the hardships of life in the Dutch

[5]   Swierenga, *Family Quarrels*, 111.

American settlements and the high mortality rates. Vander Werp had buried three wives and one child already, and Gerritdina was pregnant with their second child.[6] His own health was not robust either, so that he may not have felt led to put himself and his family in undue peril.[7]

The political situation in the United States was another matter to consider. In 1864 the Civil War was still in full force, and young Dutchmen from Michigan had signed up. Even Van Raalte's sons were serving. Vander Werp's older sons were also getting to the age that, if the war should drag on, they might be called up to serve.

With all that it is understandable that Vander Werp weighed the matter carefully. Nevertheless, when the call came a third time, he could no longer disregard it. He had to consider seriously the needs of the people so far away. Often when a pastor receives a call, he also receives letters from the calling congregation pleading for acceptance. Undoubtedly, Vander Werp received his share of letters from the United States. In this sizeable congregation there were many voices clamoring to be heard.[8] But there was one voice that Vander Werp trusted above all the others—one voice that had been with the settlers from the beginning; one voice that knew their history, their squabbles, and their needs. That voice belonged to his brother, Jan Hendrik, by now a member of the Graafschap congregation. No doubt Vander Werp recalled how thirty years before he had been the one keeping Jan Hendrik informed about that first secession; now it was Jan Hendrik who kept him informed about the American secession and how it had happened.[9]

Vander Werp packed his books, said goodbye to all that was dear to him, and at age fifty-three began a new life in a new denomination in a new country. The family crossed the ocean in September 1864. The two-week ocean voyage gave this much overworked servant of the Lord some time to pause and reflect on how the Lord had led him to this point in his life—and to ponder what God might yet require of him.

---

[6] Wilhelmina Vander Werp, born July 15, 1864, in Burum, Friesland.

[7] Wesseling, *Friesland,* 2: 246. Already in Leeuwarden, Vander Werp's health suffered occasionally from too much work. In December 1844 his consistory allowed him to decide for himself whether he was physically capable of preaching three times instead of two. He was also allowed to stay home and not travel in inclement weather.

[8] At the February 1863 congregational meeting of the Graafschap congregation, 199 ballots had been cast for an elder. Because only adult males had voting rights, this number gives us an indication of the size of the congregation.

[9] See note 179 regarding the correspondence between family members.

CHAPTER 14

Secession in Michigan

When Jan Hendrik, his wife, Cornelia, and their children left the Netherlands in March, 1847, he was still a member of the *Kruisgezinden*—the group that believed in strict adherence to the Rules of Order as established by the Synod of Dort.[1] In America, his church affiliation would take strange twists and turns, but always he would distinguish himself as a leader and be elected elder or deacon wherever he went.

After arriving in New York in early May, the family traveled by canal boat to Buffalo, from where they crossed the Great Lakes to Milwaukee. During those first summer months, with no established Reformed church nearby, the few Dutch families in the area conducted services in each other's homes on Sundays led by Jan Hendrik.[2]

Unemployment forced the family across Lake Michigan to Grand Haven after only three months in Wisconsin. In Michigan Jan Hendrik found work in the lumber mills in Nortonville, near Muskegon. But the work, driving logs to the mills and standing in water for long hours, proved too dangerous and difficult for his liking. In the spring of 1848 the family moved to the Dutch settlement of New Groningen. They

---

[1] CRC Classis Minutes, June 2, 1858, Art. 7, "daar er leden zijn in onze midden die bij de gemeente onder het kruis behoord hebben." ["There are members in our midst who used to belong to the *Kruisgezinden* congregations."] Jan Hendrik and Cornelia Vander Werp's children were Frederik, Afien, Johannes, Jan, and Maria, born in 1847, 1849, 1852, 1855, and 1860 respectively.

[2] Lucas, *Memoirs*, 141-45.

joined the Zeeland church, whose members, under the leadership of the Reverend Johannes Vander Meulen, had come from the province of Zeeland, in the southern part of the Netherlands. Even though Jan Hendrik came from the northern province of Groningen, he was soon elected elder by the congregation, which had a membership of 175 families by that time.[3]

As elder he became involved in the controversial and later much contested Union of 1850. On May 31, 1849, Isaac Wyckoff, pastor in the Reformed Church in America, the old established church founded by Dutch settlers in New Amsterdam in 1628, arrived in the Michigan colony. Representing the Board of Home Missions, he visited all the settlements and on June 4 met with the four pastors—Albertus Van Raalte, Cornelius Vander Meulen, Martin Ypma, and Seine Bolks—and a large group of colonists and discussed with them a possible union with the Reformed Church in America.[4] The three main questions voiced by Wyckoff about the beliefs and condition of the churches in the Holland Classis were taken up by a meeting of the pastors and elders later that month and afterwards shared with the congregations.[5] Subsequently, Van Raalte drew up a document stating the immigrants' position regarding creed and need and expressing a desire to live in communion with the Reformed Church. On July 10, 1849, delegates from all the churches in the classis met again in Van Raalte's home, and thirteen delegates from Zeeland, seven from Vriesland, three from Overisel, and Van Raalte from Holland signed the document, while the delegates from Graafschap, Grand Rapids, Drenthe, and South Holland abstained.[6]

---

[3]   Lucas, *Memoirs*, i, 164, 453. It may also be that he was automatically granted elder status because he had been an elder in the Netherlands. The Zeeland Church had adopted the rule that those who emigrated as elders from the Netherlands and joined the congregation should automatically continue as elder. D. H. Kromminga, *The Christian Reformed Tradition, From the Reformation to the Present* (Grand Rapids: Eerdmans, 1943), 99. Kromminga also notes that elders and deacons in the Netherlands at the time of emigration continued with common consent to hold the same offices in the new settlements in which they settled.

[4]   Beets, *De Chr. Geref. Kerk*, 69.

[5]   Lucas, *Memoirs*, I, 286.

[6]   Swierenga, *Family Quarrels*, 64. A. Van Koevering, *Legends of the Dutch* (Zeeland: Zeeland Record Co. Inc. 1960), 506. Those who signed were pastors A. C. Van Raalte, M. A. Ypma, S. Bolks, and C. Van Der Meulen and elders J. G. Van Hees, J. Hoogesteger, J. Boes, J. Kruid, J. Zijlstra, S. Kaslander, A. Van Bree, J. Van De Luyster, H. Lankheet, A. Borgers, M. Westrate, J. Kaboord, J. Vander Werp, K. J. De Vree, G. De Groot, H. O. Yntema, and G. H. Wolterink.

What prompted Jan Hendrik, certainly not a friend of Van Raalte, and stringent in his views regarding church alliance, to sign a proposed merger with the Reformed Church? Perhaps as an elder he was instructed by his congregation to do so. Perhaps he, like the others, had little knowledge of the American church and assumed it was the same as the Reformed Church had been in the Netherlands before it had lost its moorings. Perhaps he thought that without help from the East, the colony might not survive. When these churches entered into ecclesiastical fellowship with the Reformed Church in America, they were destitute and deeply appreciated the financial and other practical help from its churches in the East.[7]

Although the council minutes of the churches involved no longer exist, the proposed union was in all likelihood discussed in the various congregations in the months following. Had there been at this time a great outcry against union, there would have been ample time to halt the process, because not until May of 1850, almost a year later, did Van Raalte travel to Albany to attend the Particular Synod of the Reformed Church, carrying with him instructions to advance a union.[8] Consequently, the Reformed Church's General Synod voted to accept Classis Holland into its fellowship, and Holland Classis became part of the Reformed Church in America.

As a result of this union, Jan Hendrik and his family were members of the Reformed Church in America. However, over time he, along with some of the colonists who had joined the Secession in the Netherlands, saw some of the same maladies besetting the Reformed Church in America as they had seen in the Reformed Church in the Netherlands, even though the American church had not been touched by the reorganization of King William I in 1816.

Almost immediately there were rumblings that the union had been formed too hastily and without sufficient consideration of the actual practices within the Reformed Church. The Graafschap congregation especially had been fiercely secession-minded in the Netherlands and opposed the union. Some of their numbers began meeting separately

---

[7] Ibid., 49. The Reformed Church had also helped the first immigrants greatly in New York after their arrival. It had formed the Protestant Evangelical Holland Emigrant Society and The Netherlands Society for the Protection of Emigrants from Holland.

[8] *Classis Holland Minutes, 1848-1858* (Grand Rapids: Joint Committee of the Christian Reformed Church and the Reformed Church in America, Grand Rapids Printing Company, 1943), 36-37.

already before the union of 1850, and in 1848 against all the rules, called its own pastor.[9]

Meanwhile, Jan Hendrik made himself useful in the village of New Groningen, which had been founded by Jan Rabbers, an entrepreneur who built a sawmill on Frenchman's Creek, a tributary of the Black River. Here the settlers erected a dock to receive the baggage, food, and other necessities for the people of Zeeland and surrounding communities. They dubbed their little dock "Castle Garden," after their New York landing place.[10] As an experienced *schipper,* Jan Hendrik soon became adept at poling the flatboats through the rivers and lakes, ferrying settlers and materials. On April 30, 1851, Rabbers and another settler, Van Duren, sought permission from the classis to start a church in New Groningen. To advance their cause Rabbers stated "that their union with the Zeeland church was always meant to be a merely provisional union; that those who are weak, as well as the children, are neglected, and that there was, in the midst of them, a brother who had good gifts for edification."[11]

The classis did not approve this request, fearing that doing so would lead to all kinds of little "splinter" churches, each with its own lay leader whose preaching would be difficult to regulate—a case in point being the South Holland group which, upset about its inability to call its own minister, had split off and joined the Associate Reformed Presbyterian Church. In 1853 two-thirds of the Drenthe, Michigan, church seceded under the leadership of the Reverend Roelof H. Smit, who differed theologically with Van Raalte. It joined the Associate

---

[9]   De Haas, *Voorgangers,* 1: 241. Under the leadership of a prominent member, Harm Jan Smit, this group called K. Vander Schuur, who had a troubled ministry in the Netherlands, and who came in 1849, at the same time that Graafschap called Hendrik Klijn. Both accepted their respective calls and arrived in the colony eight days apart from each other to serve the same church, leading to great confusion and squabbles, so that Vander Schuur was asked to accept a call to Wisconsin. Swierenga, *Family Quarrels,* 68-69. In 1851 Harm Jan Smit, apparently bent on calling a pastor for the group, persuaded Jacob R. Schepers, a student of Cornelius Vander Meulen of Zeeland, to be their pastor. Under Scheper's leadership the church seceded from the Reformed Church in 1852 and became Scottish Presbyterian.

[10] Aleida J. Pieters, *A Dutch Settlement in Michigan* (Grand Rapids: The Reformed Press, 1923), 75.

[11] *Classis Holland Minutes,* 48. It is not sure who was meant by "the brother with good gifts for edification." This may have referred to Jan Hendrik Vander Werp, as he had been a leader among the *Kruisgezinden* in the Netherlands, or the schoolteacher Annerus J. Hillebrands, who began teaching in New Groningen in 1857.

Naming a Denomination

For two years, from their founding in April 1857 to February of 1859, the four seceding churches did not operate under an official name. The first statement of their first recorded classical assembly, held October 7, 1857 in Vriesland, gives an indication of their dilemma. It reads, "Since we dealt with the name we would adopt, it is decided to allow this to rest for a time." The fact that they were of one mind to unite with the *Afgescheiden* Church in the Netherlands was stated in the Polkton letter to Classis Holland. Therefore, they may have waited for affirmation of this union before naming themselves. To have joined with the *Afgescheiden* church in the Netherlands would also mean they would assume that name: *Christelijke Afgescheiden Kerk*, or Christian Seceder Church. The latter would not have been their choice, since the many *Kruisgezinden* in the group wanted to have the word "*Gereformeerd*" in the name, meaning they were part of the true church of the Synod of Dort. Two years later, when it became evident that the *Afgescheiden* in the Netherlands did not favor this union, they settled on the name *Hollandsche Gereformeerde Kerk* (Holland Reformed Church) at their February 1859 classis meeting. This did not seem to have satisfied all the brethren, for two years later still, at the February 1861 meeting, they adopted the name Free Dutch Reformed Church (without a Dutch equivalent), with "Free" meaning that they did not have to ask governmental permission to organize as the *Afgescheiden* in the Netherlands had to do. Still, this was not a unanimous decision because the Graafschap congregation held out, and not until the October 1864 meeting did they all agree on the name *Ware Hollandsche Gereformeerde Kerk*, or True Dutch Reformed Church. Graafschap's approval of this name at this particular meeting may have been due to Vander Werp's arrival and input. This name continued until 1880, when the word "True" was dropped and the word "Christian" added and the church became known as the Dutch Christian Reformed Church. When the denomination completed the change from Dutch to English, the Synod of 1936 approved dropping the "Dutch" and Christian Reformed Church became official. Because of its global outreach and the addition of many Canadian churches the Synod of 1974 added, "in North America."

Reformed Church.[12] And in 1855 Jacob Duin, an immigrant from Noordeloos, the Netherlands, formed a conventicle not far from the Vanden Bosch's Noordeloos church. Duin, though lacking in formal education, soon drew a good number of families for his worship services. He charged Van Raalte with Arminianism, claiming he, Duin, alone preached the gospel truth.[13] For the next several years the friction and fraction simmered, but would not come to a full boil until 1857.

Sometime after Classis Holland under Van Raalte's leadership joined the Reformed Church of America, and sometime before May 1852, Jan Hendrik and his family traveled to New York State, where Cornelia gave birth to their son, Johannes, in High Falls.[14] Why did Jan Hendrik travel to New York? Perhaps it was a commercial venture. As a former *schipper* he would be a suitable person to travel over the Great Lakes and Erie Canal to New York State to do business for the settlement. However, taking his family along might indicate that perhaps he meant to stay for awhile in the East to check out conditions in the Reformed Church for himself, or, again, perhaps, he wanted to learn more about the True Reformed Dutch Church, which had separated from the Reformed Church in 1822.

If indeed such was the case, then Jan Hendrik's involvement in Polkton's secession from the Reformed Church becomes more apparent. By 1854 he and his family were back in Michigan, living in Polkton, where they joined a small group of believers. This group, made up mostly of settlers from the province of Groningen (Jan Hendrik's province of origin), had been meeting in homes since their arrival late in 1849, until Cornelius Vander Meulen from Zeeland met with them and formally organized them into a church in 1854, installing elders and deacons. Jan Hendrik promptly became their leader.

As other immigrant families from the Netherlands arrived in the Michigan colonies, after having lived and worked in the East for some time, they carried with them the continued rumors that the Reformed Church was not practicing the three signs of the true church—the true preaching of the Word, the true administration of the sacraments, and the proper exercise of discipline. Other grievances included the

---

[12]   Swierenga, *Family Quarrels*, 72-75. Commonly known as the *Schotse Kerk*. Smit, trained by De Cock in the Netherlands, adhered to the northern party of the Seceders and thereby was already prejudiced against Van Raalte.

[13]   Swierenga, *Family Quarrels*, 76.

[14]   R. H. Harms, ed., *Historical Directory of the Christian Reformed Church* (Grand Rapids: CRC Publications, 2004), 354.

Albertus C. Van Raalte

complaint that the Reformed Church sang man-inspired hymns rather than the psalms, no longer preached the catechism, and allowed its members to associate with Freemasonry.

Many of these complaints were fueled by letters church members in the Michigan colonies received from a small church body, the True Reformed Dutch Church, which had seceded from the Reformed Church in 1822. These letters were then read in the churches. William Van Eyck asserts that there were close connections between the leaders of the True Reformed Dutch Church in the East and members of the Holland classis. For instance, Van Eyck reported that Rabbers of New Groningen received several letters from the East stating that the Reformed Church was not the true church.[15] Given Jan Hendrik's sojourn in the East and his close ties to Rabbers, he would have been

---

[15]   Wm. O. Van Eyck, *Landmarks of the Reformed Fathers* (Grand Rapids: The Reformed Press, 1922), 203.

aware of these letters as well.[16]

In Michigan Koene Vanden Bosch, a newly arrived Seceder pastor from the Netherlands, criticized the Union of 1850 from the moment of his arrival in the colony in 1856, adding his voice to the chorus of those opposing Van Raalte, whom some called "the pope of Holland."[17]

To his credit Van Raalte tried to smooth the ruffled feathers. In May 1856 he preached in Graafschap, where he had been invited by an elder to restore relationships.[18] It was not to be.

The most grievous words mentioned as reason number five in the Graafschap church's letter of Secession, and which may well have caused many to support the schism, were that the Secession of 1834 in the Netherlands need not to have happened.[19] Many settlers had suffered fines and persecution for the sake of the Secession in the Netherlands and were upset to hear that it had not been all that necessary. Members of the Graafschap congregation especially had suffered more severely and for a longer period in Bentheim under German (Kingdom of Hanover) authority than their Dutch counterparts, and for them these words may have seemed a final insult.[20]

In April, 1857, the Reverend Koene Vanden Bosch of Noordeloos and another pastor, Hendrik Klijn of Grand Rapids, together with members of four congregations (Noordeloos, Polkton, Grand Rapids, and Graafschap) decided by majority vote to withdraw from the Reformed Church in America and return to an independent status. Vriesland joined them soon after.[21] Jan Hendrik led the Polkton

---

16   Beets, *De Chr. Geref. Kerk*, 83. Beets characterizes Rabbers as "very influential." See also H. Brinks, "Church History via Kalamazoo 1850-1860," *Origins*, 16/1 (1998): 36-42. Brinks relates the extensive letter writing that existed and that these letters were often circulated for all to read.

17   Henry E. Dosker, *Levensschets van Rev. A. C. Van Raalte, Uit oorspronkelijke bronnen bewerkt* (Nijkerk: Callenbach, 1893), 178. J. Van Hinte, *Netherlanders in America*, 362. Even Van Raalte's best friend and coworker admitted that Van Raalte could at times be domineering and highhanded.

18   Paulus den Bleijker Papers, Calvin College Archives. Letter written by Jacob Duim to Paulus den Bleijker, May 14, 1856.

19   Swierenga, *Family Quarrels*, 85. *Classis Holland Minutes*, 242.

20   R. T. Kuiper, *Een Tijdwoord betrekkelijk de kerkelijke toestanden in Noord-Amerika* (Wildervank: Van Halteren, 1882), 9. See also Gerrit Jan Beuker, "German Oldreformed Emigration: Catastrophe or Blessing?" *Breaches and Bridges: Reformed Subcultures in the Netherlands, Germany, and the United States*, George Harinck & Hans Krabbendam, eds. (Amsterdam: VU Uitgeverij, 2000), 102-103.

21   Ibid., 82.

group to join this secession. The letter he signed stated in part, "We have betaken ourselves to the standpoint we had when we left the Netherlands, in order thus again to be in relationship with the [Seceding] Church of the Netherlands." The letter was presented to Classis Holland meeting in Zeeland April 8, 1857.[22] The four seceding congregations named the newly formed denomination the *Hollandsche Gereformeerde* Church (Holland Reformed Church).[23] As noted earlier, that the word *Gereformeerde* became part of the name was no doubt due to the influence of the *Kruisgezinden* among those who seceded.[24] It was this one word that they had fought so hard, though unsuccessfully, to keep in their name in the Netherlands.

On February 3, 1858, Jan Hendrik attended the classis meeting in Grand Rapids, representing Polkton, and closed the meeting with prayer.[25] That same year he moved to Grand Haven. The Polkton group dwindled rapidly after he left, and a few years later reverted back to holding church meetings in someone's home. In the meantime, Jan Hendrik joined the group in Grand Haven, which fared not much better. The few families that settled in Grand Haven went along with Van Raalte and organized a Reformed church in 1850. But some members were not happy with that choice and joined the Spring Lake Presbyterian Church after it was organized in 1853. This too did not last. In 1855 they formed their own independent group.[26]

After an initial spurt of growth, the group dwindled to about four families who met in each other's homes on Sundays. They would read a sermon and sing psalms, but, without an ordained person, they could not baptize or serve Communion. In October 1858 they sent a delegate to the Christian Reformed Church classis meeting, requesting that Vanden Bosch and an elder visit Grand Haven to baptize their children, who had been born in the intervening years.[27] Four years later Vanden Bosch still had not done so. At the February 5, 1862, meeting in Graafschap, Derk Sjerda, delegate from Grand Haven, insisted that

---

[22] For a complete text of all four letters see *Classis Holland Minutes*, 240-43.
[23] There were several name changes over the years (see side bar). To avoid confusion, I will use the term Christian Reformed Church throughout.
[24] CRC Classis Minutes, June 2, 1858.
[25] Ibid., February 3, 1858.
[26] J. H. Kromminga, "A Century of Grace," *Grand Haven CRC 100th. Anniversary Booklet 1855-1955*.
[27] CRC Classis Minutes, October 20, 1858.

Vanden Bosch keep his promise. But the latter, involved in all kinds of other church matters, kept making excuses.[28]

This was the situation in Grand Haven when Jan Hendrik lived there, until he returned to Polkton in 1861. In the meantime the Polkton Christian Reformed Church had disbanded, so he joined the Polkton Reformed Church and was elected elder in 1862.[29] Even so, he was not happy with the church situation; he longed to join his Christian Reformed brothers and sisters. Nevertheless, there was so much division and strife among them, so much disunity and disorganization that he came to the realization that only exceptionally strong and capable leadership would save the church.[30]

Klijn had returned to the Reformed Church, leaving only the volatile Koene Vanden Bosch as sole pastor for the five Christian Reformed churches.[31] In 1863 Wilhelmus Van Leeuwen came from the Netherlands, having been called by the Grand Rapids congregation. But Van Leeuwen was not a man to bring about peace and order either. It is very well possible that as far as Jan Hendrik was concerned there was only one person who had the organizational talents, leadership ability, and communication skills needed if the church was to survive, and that was his own brother, Douwe. In 1864 Jan Hendrik moved to Graafschap, and perhaps it is not coincidental that in the same year Vander Werp received a third formal call from this congregation.

There may also be another equally logical explanation why the Graafschap congregation, made up of immigrants mostly from Bentheim who had lived geographically closer to Van Raalte's territory in the Netherlands, would choose Vander Werp, a true man of the northern wing. The Bentheimers' pastor in Europe, Jan Barend Sundag, had studied with De Cock in Groningen. In 1840 De Cock joined Sundag in Bentheim to organize the congregation. Sundag, an outspoken opponent of Van Raalte, no doubt influenced his congregation, and once in America they looked for another De Cock disciple.[32] Vander

---

28   Ibid., February 5, 1862.

29   Loren Lemmen, "The Early Church at Polkton, Michigan," *Origins,* 12/2, (1994): 39-42.

30   Beets, *De Chr. Geref. Kerk,* 123-27.

31   *Gedenkboek Vijftigjaar Jubileum Chr. Geref. Kerk A. D. 1857-1907* (Grand Rapids: Semi-Centennial Committee, 1907), 246. Vanden Bosch is described as lacking tact, hard, rude, and short-tempered.

32   Helenius De Cock Collection, Calvin College Archives, Letter of Call dated July 23, 1851. In fact the congregation had called De Cock's son Helenius in 1851 also because "your father's name is close to our hearts."

Werp's successor, Roelof Kuiper, pointed out that "Ds. Vander Werp was the right man for the right place. Because the Graafschappers were known to be ultra orthodox, and because Ds. Vander Werp's theology could not be faulted, they deemed his preaching excellent. God's people were built up and refreshed in the faith, young people converted, and many a soul was brought to the Lord."[33]

If the Graafschap people were happy with their new pastor, Jan Hendrik must have been even more so. After a separation of seventeen years, one can only imagine the joy these two brothers experienced when they met again face to face. Jan Hendrik's familiarity with this new land and his intimate knowledge of the church situation gave Vander Werp a decided advantage for beginning his ministry in a new setting. Gerritdina, meeting these in-laws for the first time, may have been surprised at Cornelia's sun-tanned face and sun-bleached hair—so unlike her own Dutch pale skin and covered hair. Nevertheless, Gerritdina too, accepted this experienced pioneer woman's support and practical help with gratitude as she tried to make a home for her family in this new land.

---

[33]   R. T. Kuiper, *Tijdwoord*, 22.

CHAPTER 15

Graafschap, Michigan

In 1863 your father received a call from Graafschap, Michigan, in the United States. He declined the call twice and after receiving it the third time he accepted it. In September 1864, we made the long trip to America. The things that happened at our arrival and after, you have heard from us upon many occasions. You know them as well as I do. Your father was a rich blessing to many through his preaching. The Graafschap people were always very precious to me. What we experienced there is unforgettable.[1]

When, toward the end of her life, Gerritdina wrote about her life's experiences, she assumed that her children knew the stories of their first years in America and for that reason she did not write about them. We will, therefore, have to rely on extant church records to discover at least part of the story of their experiences in Graafschap. Among the members of their new congregation, besides the Bentheimers, were also many people from the province of Drenthe, and there may have been some who even remembered Vander Werp from his younger days, when, full of youthful vigor, he had served as a lay pastor in their province.[2]

---

[1] Gerritdina Vander Werp-Lokker Collection, Calvin College Archives. Gerritdina in a letter to her children dated April 29, 1903.

[2] Helenius De Cock Collection, Calvin College Archives. At the time of immigration in 1847, seventy came from Bentheim and thirty-four from Drenthe. By 1864 the makeup of the congregation as far as region of origin had probably changed somewhat, because in 1851 Jan Rutgers, elder, wrote to Helenius De Cock, "Our

Douwe J. Vander Werp

The family arrived in the colony in late September 1864, during one of the most beautiful months in Michigan, when the weather turns crisp and clear, and the trees burst into full autumn glory. The Graafschap settlement, seventeen years old when the Vander Werps arrived, had been founded by a group of immigrants largely from Bentheim County, Germany.[3] These people were acquainted with Van Raalte and the Secessionists in the Netherlands and were also seeking religious freedom. They had intended to travel with the Van Raalte party, but due to circumstances left half a year later in April 1857, arriving in the colony in June. Van Raalte, being too ill at the time to help them, advised them to settle in what is now the village of Graafschap. There they erected shanties and held worship services in the home of William Notting, a shoemaker. Whenever possible they would walk to the Holland colony and worship at Van Raalte's church.

Van Raalte ministered to both the Holland and the Graafschap people for the first year, but by the fall of 1848 the Graafschappers had

congregation is called Graafschap because the first settlers came from that area. However, now there are people from all the provinces of the Netherlands, especially from Zeeland, Overijssel, and Drenthe."

[3] For a history of the Graafschap settlement see Swenna Harger and Loren Lemmen, *The County of Bentheim and her Emigrants to America* (Holland, Mich.: privately printed, 1990).

built a simple log structure and called Hendrik Klijn from Utrecht, the Netherlands, to be their pastor. Used to city life, Klijn soon became discouraged by the primitive living conditions—with a log cabin as the church, and a lean-to as the parsonage—and after only one year accepted a call to Milwaukee.[4] He fully expected the small group in Graafschap to fold and flee the wilderness as well.[5] But they didn't. They called Seine Bolks, who had arrived from Hellendoorn, province of Overijssel, with a group of settlers. But Bolks also foresaw problems with the accommodations and with the diversity of the two groups and founded his own community in what is now Overisel, Michigan. From 1852 to 1855, Martin Ypma led the Graafschap church and then he too moved on.

For most of the next decade the congregation carried on without a pastor yet experienced a steady growth in membership. By the time the Vander Werps arrived, a new church building had been erected and a proper parsonage built. Perhaps because the latter was not large enough to house the growing family, it came up for discussion in the council three years later in September 1867. However sparse the accommodations may have been, the view from the new parsonage was spectacular.

Some fifteen years later, Roelof Kuiper would write,

> When I look out from my study and survey the country on every side of our hill, which rises 150 feet above the water level of Lake Michigan, my eye nowhere sees any woods. It is a free and spacious view we have of the thousands of fruitful acres and hundreds of white painted houses and roomy barns standing beside them in the midst of these fields. A beautiful sight, especially in the summer, when the billowing wheat and other crops cover these acres; and pleasing indeed is the view of lush meadows with cattle pasturing in them.[6]

Vander Werp's installation in Graafschap took place Sunday, October 9, 1864. Immediately, one old habit from the Netherlands met its death knell. When he stepped out of his study that Sunday morning

---

[4]   Graafschap CRC Minutes, September 10, 1849, and October 29, 1850. Klijn may also have been concerned about the health of his wife in such primitive settings. She is described as being an invalid in Lucas, *Memoirs*, 431.

[5]   Kuiper, *Tijdwoord*, 15.

[6]   R. T. Kuiper, *A Voice from America about America* (Grand Rapids: Eerdmans, 1970), 44.

wearing *het ambtsgewaad*, the standard clerical attire he had worn in the
Netherlands—the knickers, long coat, white bib tie, and three-cornered
hat—the maid took one look at the outfit and shrieked at the strange
sight. Vander Werp hastened back into the house, changed his clothes,
and never wore the old costume again.[7] When Van Leeuwen proposed
the continued wearing of this clergy garb at a classis meeting, he found
himself out-voted. The out-dated, eighteenth-century costume met
the same fate as the regional Dutch costumes of the women—they
were buried in old trunks in attics.[8] One item that kept its usefulness,
however, was the wooden shoe. The wearing of this typical Dutch
footwear, called *klompen*, continued for almost fifty years. A handful of
straw not only helped the *klompen* fit snuggly, but also kept a person's
feet warm. Settlers tacked their cloth leggings onto the *klompen* for
protection against snow and dirt in the wintertime—and like their
contemporaries in the old country, they left their *klompen* outside the
door when they entered a house.[9]

The two older Vander Werp children, Jan, sixteen, and Catherine,
fourteen, had finished their grade school education. Dirk, three, and
baby Wilhemina were too young for school, leaving only Reinder,
eleven, to attend school in America.

Much of the joy and excitement of beginning a new ministry in
a new land in the new year of 1865 was overshadowed by the news that
Johannes, Vander Werp's oldest, and his only son by his first wife, had
passed away December 27, 1864, in Amsterdam. On the death certificate
Johannes's occupation is listed as *dragonder*, a member of the military's
cavalry division.[10]

When on May 25, 1866, Gerritdina gave birth to a son—their first
child to be born in America—they named the child Johannes, ensuring,
as was customary among the Dutch, that the grandfather's name
continue. Many years later, this American-born Johannes would be

7   M. J. Vanderwerp, "Rev. Douwe Johannes Vander Werp, Eerste Hoofredacteur," *De
     Wachter,* Feb. 6, 1968, 6.
8   There is an interesting story in Dingeman Versteeg, *De Pelgrim Vaders van het Westen*
     (Grand Rapids: C. M. Loomis & Co.) 18, 72. Vander Meulen walked around with
     a very funny looking felt hat and when asked where he got it, he said it was his
     tri-cornered Dutch preaching hat from which he had loosened the three corners,
     giving him a wide brim for sunshade.
9   John H. Boven and Carol G. Boven, *Boven Dutch Apple Pie* (Wyandotte, Okla.:
     Gregath, n.d.), 19.
10   Amsterdam Civil Registry of deaths 1864. Family History Library, Salt Lake City,
     International Film #253,828.

admitted to the bar at age twenty-one and elected judge of probate in 1896, becoming a state senator from 1911-1912.[11] Gerritdina's recovery from this birth was slow. At the June 6, 1866, classis meeting, Vander Werp reports his inability to travel to Grand Haven to lead a worship service there due to his wife's continued infirmity.

Vander Werp had been called at a salary of $400 per year, plus free firewood and free housing. From his income he had to feed, clothe, and educate his growing family. Besides the five children they had when they came to America, they had three more during their years in Graafschap. The household also included Gerritdina's elderly mother.[12] That the family's budget was stretched to the limit is reflected by the fact that two and half years after coming to America Vander Werp still had outstanding travel debts, which he promised to pay as soon as he was able.[13]

In 1862 the congregation had built a new church edifice, which replaced the old log structure from the early pioneer days. Just how finished it was in at the time Vander Werp arrived is difficult to assess, because Lambertus Scholte writes, "The present imposing church structure commanding a wide view of the Graafschap countryside was finished during the early years of his [Vander Werp's] pastorate."[14]

Perhaps Vander Werp oversaw some of the finishing of the interior. The minutes of Graafschap note that in the midst of the winter of 1866, Jan Hendrik Vander Werp traveled to Grand Rapids to "negotiate the

---

[11] *Muskegon Chronicle*, August 11, 1939. "State Senator John Vanderwerp, 73, long active in state and civic affairs here, died Friday at his home after suffering a heart attack. Mr. Vanderwerp, a lifelong Republican, was elected state senator last fall. He had served previously in that capacity in 1911 and 1912. Previous to that time he was judge of probate, but had resigned to become senator. After serving his first term as senator he was elected to the circuit court bench and served 18 years before retiring from the bench in 1936. Actively engaged in the practice of law for 51 years, Mr. Vanderwerp was the oldest practicing lawyer in Muskegon County. At the time of his death he was attorney for the board of education. Mr. Vanderwerp was a trustee of Hope College, which honored him with an honorary degree."

[12] Gerritdina's parents came to America with the Vander Werps in 1864; her father passed away shortly after their arrival; her mother continued to live with the family.

[13] Graafschap CRC Minutes, January 17, 1867. It seemed that Vander Werp still owed money to Arie Vander Waal. Perhaps he spent more than the stipulated amount for personal belongings, books, etc., or perhaps he had to pay for his in-laws who traveled with him.

[14] Lucas, *Memoirs*, 98.

Walking to Graafschap Church in the wintertime

construction of a pulpit with DeGraaf Brothers. It was to be picked up on two wagons, or sleds in the event of heavy snow, at a cost of $100, or less"—a hefty sum in those days. Jan Hendrik also negotiated that the painting of the primer coat be done by the DeGraaf Brothers, while he would apply the finish coat himself once the pulpit was in its proper place. From the size and price of the pulpit, we may assume that it had some of the same features as those of the Reformed churches in the Netherlands. When, a little later in the same year, the question arose at classis if an elder reading a sermon might also use the pulpit, the answer was no—"no unordained person may use the pulpit."[15]

This ruling would also affect Jan Hendrik who, according to the minutes of October 26, 1869, had been selected as the *voorzanger.* Thus many a time the Vander Werp brothers led the worship service together. From January 1870 until November of that same year, Jan Hendrik also served as clerk for the Graafschap consistory, and for those months Vander Werp, who recorded the minutes, also signed them as D. J. v. d. Werp, president, and J. H. v. d. Werp, clerk.[16] The two signatures are so similar that it is most likely Vander Werp signed for his brother. On two occasions—August 1870 in Holland, Michigan, and June 1871 in

[15]   CRC Classis Minutes, September1866.
[16]   Graafschap CRC Minutes, January 1870 through November 1870.

A horse and buggy ride to a church meeting

Chicago—the brothers served as pastor and elder delegate at the same classis meeting.[17]

Not only did the pulpit have significance, but seating was also according to status. Elders and deacons sat on raised benches at the front of the sanctuary, flanking and facing the pulpit, while the men and boys sat separately from the women and children in the pews. During Communion services, the men were served first, then the women.[18]

An important feature added to the church building during Vander Werp's years in Graafschap was the bell. This bell, which rang at seven o'clock in the morning, at noon, and again at six o'clock in the evening, regulated the working hours for farmers and villagers. On Sundays the bell rang an hour and one-half hour before both services. For funerals, a special muted clapper tolled once for each year of the deceased's life. No doubt the pealing of the bell brought comfort to many settlers as it reminded them of their old country village church bell.[19]

A few years after arriving in Graafschap, Vander Werp's workload included taking on the training of students for the ministry. Because it had been unsuccessful in recruiting ordained ministers from the

[17]   CRC Synodical Minutes 1857-1880.
[18]   Robert P. Swierenga, *Dutch Chicago: A History of the Hollanders in the Windy City* (Grand Rapids: Eerdmans, 2002), 110.
[19]   Lucas, *Memoirs*, 98-99.

Netherlands, the classis already in February 1861 had raised the possibility of training its own pastors.[20] However, not until Van Leeuwen consented to teach John Schepers in October 1864 did a training program get under way. When Van Leeuwen accepted a call to Paterson, New Jersey, in 1867, Schepers continued his studies with Vander Werp, who had been assigned the task of training Harm Lukas at the classis meeting of April 1865. Harm Lukas did not complete his studies, but John Schepers was ordained in 1868. In 1869 the classis decided that Vander Werp should do all the training until the church could afford to establish a seminary.

In a letter written January 30, 1867, Vander Werp described his situation to his erstwhile friend, the Reverend Dirk Postma, who had emigrated and organized an *Afgescheiden* church in South Africa.[21]

> I am busy here night and day. For a year now I have been training two students, and now a third one has been added. I am constantly invited to preach and organize new congregations; I receive many letters from all over that need to be answered; besides that I have a large congregation of more than two hundred and fifty members, who live in a three mile radius around the church, and then there is the care for the other congregations who are still without a shepherd.[22]

---

[20]   CRC Classis Minutes, February, 1861. *Semi-Centennial Volume Theological School and Calvin College 1876-1926* (Grand Rapids: The Semi-centennial Committee, 1926), 21. The primary reasons Dutch pastors resisted coming to the United States was because they were "loath to come to this continent to help the so-called Seceders, not understanding the situation in America." Also, the CRC had been unable to establish ecclesiastical fellowship with the *Afgescheiden* Church in the Netherlands.

[21]   Dirk Postma Collection, The Library of the Gereformeerde Kerk, Potchefstroom, Vander Werp to Postma, letter dated January 30, 1867. Dirk Pieters Postma (1818-1890) was born in Dokkum, Friesland. He was trained by Tamme F. De Haan and served *Afgescheiden* churches in Minnertsga, Middelstum, Bedum, Wildervank, and Zwolle. In 1858, he was deputized by the synod to travel to South Africa on a fact-finding mission as well as to do mission work. He stayed in South Africa, where he organized the *Gereformeerde Kerk* of South Africa, trained students, and founded a seminary.

[22]   Ibid. "Ik heb hier bijna nacht en dag werk. Al over een jaar heb ik twee studenten nu is er een derde bij gekomen, overal roept men om te komen prediken en nieuwe gemeenten te stichten, van alle oorden krijg ik brieven die beantwoord moeten worden, en ik heb een groote gemeente van meer dan twee honderd vijftig ledematen, die zoo wat drie mijlen in het ronde van de kerk wonen en dan de zorg der overige gemeenten van onze kerk die nog herderloos zijn."

Blacksmith shop in Graafschap, Michigan

Three and a half years later, in a letter to friends in Burum, the Netherlands, dated August 8, 1871, Gerritdina mentions three of the students—Eppe van der Vries, Berend Mollema, and William Hellenthal—whom Vander Werp was instructing at the time. The letter also shows that Gerritdina herself was clearly overworked at home.[23]

> For a while I was very depressed because of our large housekeeping. We have five little children. My mother has been ill as well and is still very weak. The maid has her hands full. I used to be able to do so much more, but lately I am so tired. I also have a bad rash on my arms and hands, so bad I cannot sew or knit.

About her husband's health she wrote, "*Dominee* suffers from rheumatism, but still tries to do his work with cheerfulness." Another letter written a day later to other friends in Burum provides a snapshot of the family. She wrote,

> You probably heard that Jan and Kaatje are both married.[24] Jan is a farmer and is doing well. Those willing to work hard, can with God's blessing get ahead here. They had a little daughter, but she only got to be five months old before she died. They live close by us, just about as far as Visvliet is from Burum.[25] Kaatje is married

23 Vander Werp-Lokker Collection, Calvin College Archives.
24 Jan married Jacoba Van Zanten on Sept. 23, 1869; Jacoba passed away in 1873 at age twenty-one.
25 Approximately two kilometers.

to [the] Reverend [Leonard] Rietdijk and lives in Muskegon. That is about a three-hour train ride away from us and every time we have a Classis meeting, she comes along with her husband and they stay with us. They have one little son who is presently sick. We hope that he soon will be well again. Reinder lives with and works for a farmer about half an hour away from us. He has really grown big and heavy. He is already bigger than the Reverend. Those are the three oldest children; then we still have five little ones. Dirk, the oldest, is ten. Mina turned seven this past summer. She was eight weeks when we left Burum. Johannes is five. He is already a real American—a healthy, solid boy. Douwe is three and our little William is one. So, three are Americans. Oh, that the Lord in his mercy may be praised through our many children is our prayer. We always enjoyed having Kaatje around. I really missed her at first after she married. Still that was the path she had to take and sooner or later we would have had to let her go. She has a fine believing husband and we may also believe that about her, so great blessings, right? We talk much about you and our other old friends. Three of our students, Eppe van der Vries, Berend Mollema and Willem Hellenthal are from your area—Niezijl and Grijpskerk.[26]

Vander Werp added a few lines at the bottom of the same letter.

Dear friends,
May the Lord have mercy on us for this time and for eternity. You are probably unhappy with me for not writing, although I will never forget you. If you only knew how busy I am here in America. I came here at the right time and am being blessed not just materially, but especially in spiritual and church matters. Last week I bought a farm for Reinder for twelve hundred dollars. The farm already had twenty-five acres cleared and planted. Four of my students are already pastors and are working with blessing and the four I have now are also already preaching. Our own health is up and down, especially my dear wife's ailments. Nevertheless, we are often aware how here in America the Lord has

---

[26] Harms, *Historical Directory*. Eppe (Edward) Vander Vries (1844-1923) was ordained in 1874 and served six CRC churches; Berend (Bernard) Mollema was also ordained in 1874 and served five CRC churches; Willem Hellenthal, the only student who had studied classical languages, was sent to the Netherlands to finish his education and passed away shortly upon his arrival.

been good to us. We are learning to die to this life so we can live for the Lord. Everything this world has to offer is becoming less and less in our eyes and Christ is becoming all and all. The tests and trials we experience are profitable, because through them our life is strengthened in the communion and service of the Lord. I could write much to you, but my wife has already written quite a bit, and my other duties call me. You have no idea how busy I am here. At sixty years of age, I am really too busy; I cannot keep up with it all. Please greet all our friends and share both letters with each other. Greetings from your former pastor, D v d W.[27]

Vander Werp's health remained a concern. Three years before these letters were written, in the October 9, 1868, issue of *De Wachter*, Vander Werp already described his own health as sickly, accompanied

---

One Church's Expenses for a Pastor

On December 17, 1867, Vander Werp signed a Letter of Call inviting the Reverend J. Petersen, from Heemse in the Netherlands, to become pastor of the Niekerk, Michigan, CRC. (Vander Werp had formally organized the Niekerk church September 15, 1866.) The letter offered Petersen, besides the voyage across, free living in the parsonage, free firewood, three acres of land, and $500 annually. Petersen apparently declined because, on October 26, 1868, Sietze Baron, a pastor in Bergum, Friesland, received the call and accepted it. His travel expenses came to 220 guilders per family member for the boat trip, and 32.25 guilders per person for the train from New York to Grand Rapids. These costs excluded the fee for transporting goods. The church sent Baron a voucher for $600, which equaled 940 guilders. He would be remunerated for any travel cost not covered by the $600. The parsonage, he was told, had been furnished and stocked with food. The Baron family traveled from Harlingen, Friesland to Rotterdam, and from there to New York. They arrived at Castle Garden, booked passage to Grand Rapids, where some members of the Niekerk church were waiting with wagons to pick them up. (Sietse Baron, Immigrant Papers Collection, Calvin College Archives.)

---

[27] Vander Werp-Lokker Collection, Calvin College Archives.

by all the weaknesses associated with aging. So much so that he no longer felt it worth his while to engage in polemics in the paper he edited.[28]

In spite of the overwhelming workload and physical woes, there were also cheerful times in the parsonage. Vander Werp's grandson remembered,

> One of his students had advanced enough in his studies that grandfather asked him to make and preach a sermon. This sermon would be preached in grandfather's presence only, in the privacy of grandfather's study. The student began to preach, but after a while found it so silly to be preaching to only one person, that he broke out in laughter, and grandfather laughed heartily along with him.[29]

Twice a week the students came to the Graafschap parsonage, where Vander Werp instructed them in practical theology, Bible history, geography and chronology, church history, Dutch language, exegesis, and preaching. Their textbooks included A. Francken's *Kern der Christelijke Leere [Core of the Christian Doctrine]*.[30] This text, a compendium of a larger work of three volumes on systematic theology, was written in the form of questions with answers that were to be memorized.

Vander Werp taught his students the same preaching methods he had been taught by De Cock and De Haan. First one needed to exegete the biblical text, and then apply that text in a fitting *toepassing*, or application, to encourage and uplift the believer and admonish the unbeliever. When the Reformation introduced the sermon, it immediately became the focal point of the worship service. Algra summed it up this way, "The main purpose of the service is the sermon; all the rest is secondary. People come to church to hear the sermon."[31] One of the reasons why so many people flocked to conventicles to hear uneducated lay preachers preach instead of the educated pastors in their Reformed churches was because they missed the experiential note in the sermons of these pastors. People wanted to be assured that the messenger had lived and breathed the message he brought. These

---

[28]   *De Wachter,* October 9, 1858.
[29]   Marvin J. Vander Werp, "Rev. Douwe Johannes Vander Werp, Eerste Hoofdredacteur," *De Wachter,* Feb. 6 1968, 6-7.
[30]   Beets, *Chr. Geref. Kerk,* 148.
[31]   Algra, *Wonder,* 272

Gerritdina

people who had experienced soul-wrenching conversions themselves could detect a "clanging cymbal" a mile away.

No wonder one of Vander Werp's students failed to show up when his turn came to preach. He had been extremely nervous all day and when it came time to go to church, he told the farmer with whom he was staying to just go ahead with the horse and buggy, and that he would walk to church. The people waited and waited, but no student. Finally Vander Werp spoke a few words and dismissed the congregation. The student had taken refuge in the woods until the service was over.[32]

When the students practiced their preaching to the Graafschap congregation, the elders critiqued the messages, and at one council meeting, reminded the pastor to discuss these critiques with the students for their own correction and encouragement.[33] Having his students preach occasionally provided a respite for Vander Werp, and to ease his work load further, the council also graciously released him from the house visitations.

Training these students meant Vander Werp had total control over their theological viewpoint—and indirectly the theological character of the Christian Reformed Church. In a letter to Postma he complained about the young ministers coming from the Netherlands

[32] Vander Werp, *De Wachter*, February 6, 1968, 6.
[33] Graafschap CRC Minutes, August 1871.

Anthony Brummelkamp

who had been trained at the Kampen Theological School, and who had been influenced by Professor Anthony Brummelkamp's *Remonstantse* leanings.[34] That would not happen on his watch.

With a growing and active family occupying the parsonage, as well as students coming for instruction, the council discussed the condition of the parsonage again in early 1871. Should it repair the current home or build a new one? After several weeks the decision was made to begin saving for a new parsonage and haul the lumber in the winter, when it could be transported more easily. In August of that year, Vander Werp had written to friends in Burum all was well with them, and that they were blessed in America, but the year ended in tragedy. The great fire that burned most of Holland, Michigan, in October 1871 touched the life of the Graafschap congregation as well. Although the parsonage sustained some damage, the plans to rebuild were put on hold, as no one in the congregation had the ability to pay. The money saved for lumber for the new parsonage was instead used to pay Vander Werp's

[34]   Postma Collection, letter dated January 3, 1868.

salary. The consistory also decided to write letters to churches "in the East" to ask for financial aid.[35] Since the church was not in ecclesiastical fellowship with the Reformed Church in America, it may be assumed that the consistory wrote for help to the True Reformed Dutch Church. Delegates of this latter denomination had established ecclesiastical fellowship with the True Dutch Reformed Church.[36]

[35]   Graafschap CRC Minutes, October 12, 1871.
[36]   Swierenga, *Family Quarrels*, 46. Note also the confusing similarity in names: The 1822 group that had seceded from the Reformed Church in America called itself the True Reformed Dutch Church, while the 1857 group that seceded called itself the True Dutch Reformed Church.

CHAPTER 16

Building the Walls of Zion

During his years as a pastor in the Netherlands, Vander Werp did not limit his ministry to his own congregations. Although his love for his parishioners was genuine, his heart was also firmly committed to the entire Secessionist denomination, as evidenced by the many times he served as a classical correspondent, as representative and clerk to national synods, and as trustee of the Kampen Theological School.

This pattern also held true in America. Shortly after his arrival in Graafschap Vander Werp was invited to preach for a small group of people living in the city of Holland who had broken away from Van Raalte's congregation. Three people in particular—Hellenthal, Krabshuis, and Ploeg—differed with Van Raalte. They, along with about ten other families, were meeting on their own. Walking distances from Holland to Graafschap, especially in the wintertime, prevented them from joining the Graafschap Christian Reformed congregation. Elders from the Graafschap church usually led the worship services for these people in the home of one of the families. With Vander Werp preaching regularly for them, they soon outgrew their small meeting place and asked permission to meet in the Reformed church—Van Raalte's church. This request was graciously granted, and Vander Werp was allowed to preach in the large, imposing edifice known as the Pillar Church, erected only eight years prior in 1856.[1]

---

[1] B. De Beij and A. Zwemer, *Stemmen uit de Hollandsch-Gereformeerde Kerk in de Vereenigde Staten van Amerika* (Groningen: G. J. Reits, 1871), 153.

However, according to B. De Beij and A. Zwemer, "Rev. Vander Werp acted dishonorably."[2] He did not use the pulpit of his benefactors to establish collegial fellowship with his Reformed Church brothers but instead encouraged his hearers in their opposition, spoke ill of the professors at the Kampen Theological School and sided with those who contested the renting out of pews in the Pillar Church. This last complaint—rental of church pews—had until this time not been a problem for Vander Werp, who came out of a tradition in the Netherlands where pew rental was the most common way for churches to finance their expenses.[3]

One year later, on November 8, 1865, Vander Werp organized the group as a congregation, and Market Street Christian Reformed Church (now Central Avenue Christian Reformed Church) came into existence. Vander Werp continued on as counselor until the Reverend Johan De Beer arrived in May of 1867. However, the congregation's continual internal strife caused De Beer to leave in October of the same year.[4] This left Vander Werp to pastor two congregations besides his work for the classis until the Reverend Frederick B. Hulst arrived from the Netherlands in 1868.

Appreciated as he generally was, not everyone in the Graafschap congregation agreed with Vander Werp's theology. At the consistory meeting of January 15, 1866, one of the members of the congregation accused him of Labadism with regard to membership. The matter was not settled at that meeting, for the same accusation arose again two months later at the March 14 meeting.[5] It was not the first time that Vander Werp had heard this accusation.

It had been raised before in the Netherlands by the Reformed minister J. W. Felix in Heeg, Friesland. Felix, an orthodox pastor and one of the founding members of the Frisian Réveil, decried the schism the Seceders had caused in the Reformed Church, which he considered the public church of the Netherlands.[6] According to Felix, the Seceders

---

[2] Ibid., 153. "Heeft ds. van der Werp onedelijk gehandeld." Because *Stemmen* was published in 1871, Vander Werp in all likelihood must have heard of it and possibly read for himself how others viewed his actions.

[3] See chapter 10.

[4] Johan Boelens De Beer (1819-1891). De Beer not only left Market Street, he left the CRC and joined the RCA.

[5] Graafschap CRC Minutes, January 15, 1866 and March 14, 1866. Frederick B. Hulst (1827-1873) stayed only three years. He served First Chicago from 1871 until his death in 1873.

[6] See chapter 11, Ferwerd and Lioessens. The Réveil was made up of orthodox-minded

had fallen into the trap of Labadism, the sect that only welcomed the elect in their community of believers. Labadists, followers of Jean de Labadie, a converted Roman Catholic Jesuit priest, believed that the true church consisted only of the elect. Unbelievers did not belong in the church, and the children of God could have no fellowship with the children of the world. The minister and fellow believers had the right to decide who was "elect" and who was not. Rigid discipline was enforced and members had to confess their sins, even their sinful thoughts, to one another.[7] Although the sect had died out, strains of this particular view of church membership surfaced persistently in Dutch religious thought.[8] It had even been raised by De Cock's group, the northern wing of the *Afgescheiden*, when they accused Scholte, who believed that only children of professing members should be baptized, of labadism.[9] To be accused of Labadism, therefore, meant that Vander Werp had enforced strict church discipline in Graafschap, and those wishing to join the congregation had to sustain a thorough examination as to their knowledge, faith, and Christian walk. For instance, when five young people came to make profession of faith at the March 14, 1866, council meeting, four were accepted as members, but one was not even though she was considered spiritually sound, because she was simple minded and found to be weak in knowledge. At the same meeting several other members were disciplined and not allowed to partake of Communion.

---

members of the Reformed Church who did not want to secede but rather work to reform the church from within. They were also active in society by combating alcoholism, abolishing slavery, assisting the poor, establishing orphanages and homes for unwed mothers.

[7]   Jean de Labadie (1610 – 1674) was born in France and became a Roman Catholic Jesuit priest serving churches in Bordeaux, Paris, and Amiens. He converted to Protestantism in 1650 and in 1659 served the Reformed church in Geneva. In 1666 he became pastor of the *Waalse* (French speaking) church in Middelburg, the Netherlands, where he soon came in conflict with their synod. Denying its authority over him, he left the synod and formed an independent group, which recognized as members only those who had been "born again." After his death his followers founded a commune in Wieuwerd, Friesland where they practiced that only those who could testify to having been born again would be allowed membership. Married couples were encouraged to leave a spouse who did not agree with the group's theology. See also C. van Rijswijk, *De Poorten Sions bemind boven alle woningen Jacobs* (Zwijndrecht, Van den Berg, 1983), 30-34.

[8]   Algra, *Wonder*, 97.

[9]   Bouwman, *Crisis der Jeugd*, 16, 23.

The council also excommunicated the member who accused Vander Werp of Labadism.[10]

The Labadism controversy in the Graafschap church coincided with a major event happening in the colony. In January 1866 Albert Clapper, a Methodist Episcopalian lay preacher, felt called by God to "save" Holland, and began to hold religious services. As his crowds grew Clapper, too, asked permission to use the First Reformed Church—Pillar Church—and he too was allowed to preach from Van Raalte's pulpit. In spite of the winter weather many people from all social and religious backgrounds filled the church, listened to Clapper, sang popular hymns, and prayed together.[11] Did these revival meetings remind Vander Werp of the early days of the *Afscheiding* when people traveled great distances to hear De Cock preach, and of his own days as a fiery young lay preacher stirring his hearers? Did he encourage his people to attend and be uplifted in the faith? Or did he warn his flock against the influence of this man whose religious viewpoints differed from the True Reformed? Was his stand against the revival preacher perhaps the cause of the accusation of Labadism?

No sooner had the Clapper revival run its course when another matter took center stage. In April 1866 Van Raalte and his wife, Christine, traveled to the Netherlands, and while there Van Raalte addressed the synod of the *Afgescheiden* Church on May 31, in Amsterdam, and was invited to be seated as an advising delegate. When, near the end of the synod on June 8, he was questioned about the 1857 split, Van Raalte answered that it had been due to certain [negative] elements who had arrived from the Netherlands, and he hoped with God's blessing that these misguided and schismatic people could yet be brought back into the fold.[12]

Needless to say the Christian Reformed brothers were not happy with Van Raalte's remarks. All along they had considered themselves to be the true fraternal brothers of the *Afgescheiden* Church in the Netherlands, and now they believed that they had been dealt a considerable insult.

---

[10] Graafschap CRC Minutes, March 14, 1866. Wesseling, *Friesland*, 2; 244. Vander Werp's emphasis on church discipline evidenced itself early in his ministry. At the first church he served in Leeuwarden as ordained pastor, he immediately began a rigorous schedule to visit every member before the scheduled Lord Supper services. As a result, several members were barred from the Communion table.

[11] Van Hinte, *Netherlanders*, 377-78.

[12] *Handelingen*, 965.

Dirk Postma

Vander Werp vented his indignation in a letter to Postma in South Africa.

> Now they [the *Afgescheiden* church in the Netherlands] have extended the hand of fellowship to Van Raalte and the Reformed Church in America, with all its heresies, which Van Raalte has camouflaged, and thereby condemned our secession. Previously when we asked at three separate times to be accepted, they answered that they could not judge the situation here, and declared to acknowledge all churches that held to the Reformed faith and doctrines.[13]

Was there no one at this particular synod sympathetic to the seceders in America? Were there no friends willing to plead their cause? Vander Werp's friend Kreulen with whom he had written the *Apologie* was a delegate to this synod, but unfortunately he missed the

---

[13]   Postma Collection, letter dated January 30, 1867, "Want nu heeft men Ds. Van Raalte en de Holl. Geref. Kerk met die dwalingen, die van Raalte verbloemt heeft de broederhand gegeven en ons daardoor in onze afscheiding veroordeelt. Vroeger toen wij het vanwege onze kerk drie onderscheiden malen gevraagt hebben antwoorde men het niet te kunnen beoordelen en verklaarde al de kerken te erkennen, die zich hielden aan de Geref. leer en Kerkregeering."

first day and a half due to illness. He therefore missed Van Raalte's glowing remarks about the Reformed Church in America, and probably believed he could make no judgments without having heard them. Also, unfortunately, Bernardus de Beij from Middelstum was a delegate to this synod; though he was a Groninger like Vander Werp, his opinion of the seceders in America was negative indeed.[14] When he immigrated to America in 1868 he joined the First Reformed Church in Chicago. It seems Van Raalte had won over De Beij as well.

Earlier in the letter to Postma, commenting on the [in his opinion] heterodoxy of the Reformed Church, Vander Werp noted, "And to that confused Babel Van Raalte belongs. If the secession in the Netherlands was needful, the secession here is truly crucial."[15]

Despite their rejection by the *Afgescheiden* Church in the Netherlands, the Christian Reformed tried their best to prove themselves worthy of being accepted. When *De Wachter* was published in 1868, the classis voted to send twenty-five copies of each edition to key people in the Netherlands.[16] They also worked on publishing an apology defending their secession.[17] The plan was to mail this brochure to all the consistories of the *Afgescheiden* churches in the Netherlands, hoping thereby to justify their secession to all.[18] Unfortunately it is not known if this plan was ever executed. The mother church in the Netherlands would not recognize the Christian Reformed Church in America until the 1880s, long after Vander Werp's death, when the dispute over lodge membership tilted the attitude of the mother church in favor of the Christian Reformed Church.

Another issue needing church oversight pertained to the education of the children. The minutes of the Graafschap Christian Reformed Church of April 20, 1857—just a few weeks after its

[14]   Schaap, *Family Album*, 177. H. J. Brinks, "Bernardus De Beij (1815-1894)" *Origins* 1: 1983, 9-17. De Beij was trained by Dirk Postma, a very orthodox pastor in Middelstum. In 1868 De Beij also went to America, where he joined the Reformed Church.

[15]   Ibid., "Bij dat verwarde Babel behoort van Raalte. Was de afscheiding in Nederland wettig, dan was ze hier noodzakelijk."

[16]   CRC Classis Minutes, September 2-3, 1868. Art. 20.

[17]   *Brochure op Kerkelijk Gebied, bevattende: eene ontwikkeling uit officieele bronnen van den feitelijken toestand der Reformed Protestant (Dutch) Church in America; alsmede een verdediging van de gegrondheid der "terugkeering van de Ware Hollandsche Gereformeerde Kerk in Amerika tot het oude standpunt dat men in 1849 verlaten had"* (Holland, Mich.: C. Vorst, 1869).

[18]   Postma Collection, letter dated January 30, 1867.

secession—dealt with the matter of education and finding a teacher for the children. How successful the church was is not recorded. A few years before Vander Werp's arrival, a little "Hollandsche School" had been initiated in Graafschap under the direct supervision of the church. A year and a half after Vander Werp's arrival, the church council, at the January 1866 meeting, held a long discussion on the importance of the church remaining in charge of the school. In March of the same year, G. Van Ooyen, a teacher from Burum, the Netherlands, arrived.

According to Lambertus Scholten, a pupil at the time,

> The children received instruction in the Bible, biblical history, and the three Rs—all in the Dutch language. Pupils were charged ten or twenty-five cents per month to pay the salary of the *meester*, as we called the teacher. One such teacher was *Meester* G. Van Ooyen a rather wrathy disciplinarian who had originally [like Vander Werp] come from Burum, Friesland.[19]

Gerrit Van Ooyen, described by his young pupil as "wrathy" (perhaps he meant strict), originally came from Maurik, Province of Gelderland. He taught in Burum during Vander Werp's pastorate, and very likely Vander Werp encouraged him to come teach the children in America.[20]

Home, church, and school all demanded his attention, and those three areas of concern would have been enough to keep him fully occupied, yet there was also the classis.

---

[19] L. B. Scholten, "Memories of early days in Graafschap," Lucas, *Memoirs*, 98.

[20] Graafschap CRC Minutes, March 1866. Van Ooyen was engaged for $35 per month. Later he moved to Chicago where he passed away in December 1876 at age forty-nine. See also Beets, *De Chr. Geref. Kerk*, 413.

.

CHAPTER 17

Classis Michigan

His clergy credentials having been found to be in good order, Vander Werp was formally welcomed at the classis meeting held October 12 and 13, 1864, in Graafschap. He needed no introduction to his two colleagues—Wilhelmus van Leeuwen and Koene Vanden Bosch. He had followed Van Leeuwen, a fellow Groninger, in Den Helder and knew him also from his association with the *Kruisgezinden*. Vanden Bosch hailed from the province of Drenthe and he and Vander Werp had served as delegates to the same synod in Amsterdam in 1851.[1] The three had circled in each other's orbits since their ordination in the Netherlands and now met again, very appropriately at a church meeting.[2]

Vander Werp opened the meeting with a sermon on Galatians 6:14. One of the first agenda items was to insure that the elders understood the rules of the church order, so Vander Werp commissioned the reprinting of Koelman's *Het am[b]t en de pligten der ouderlingen en diakenen*, or *The function and the duties of the elders and deacons*.[3]

A motion was made to abandon the habit of beginning the meetings with a full-length sermon. It tended to bring so many people

[1] *Handelingen,* 506.
[2] *De Wachter* Vol. 1, #18, October 9, 1868. Vander Werp writes that he (Vander Werp) was well-known both in the Netherlands and the United States.
[3] J. Koelman, *Het am[b]t en de pligten der ouderlingen en diakenen* ('s Gravenhage: van Golverdinge, 1837). This book was reprinted by T. Binnekant in Holland, Michigan, date unknown.

Wilhelmus H. Van Leeuwen

to the meeting that it often turned into a *volksvergadering*, or townhall meeting. Vander Werp wisely suggested that, rather than doing away with the sermon, it could be held at the close of the meeting so that parishioners who so wished could still attend. It was also decided to allow only those who had special permission to attend the meetings to be present.[4]

The matter of a name came up in the afternoon session. The classis adopted the name, *Ware Hollandse Gereformeerde Kerk* (True Dutch Reformed Church), when Graafschap, heretofore a holdout but now represented by Vander Werp, accepted the name. The name had Vander Werp's stamp of approval; had he perceived the word "true" (which even his nephew, the Reverend Henry Vander Werp, called "reactionary") as problematic, it would not have passed.[5] But in this matter, Vander Werp again showed his consistent agreement with De Cock's views who, until his death, proclaimed adamantly that the *Afgescheiden* constituted the "true" and the Reformed Church the "false" church.[6]

---

[4]   At a subsequent meeting it was decided not to continue publishing the minutes of the meetings in the public press as had been the custom, because it tended to generate squabbles.

[5]   Henry Vander Werp, *An Outline of the History of the Christian Reformed Church of America* (Holland, Mich.: Holkeboer, 1898), 38.

[6]   E. G. van Teylingen, "Eenige Opmerkingen over de snelle verbreiding van de afscheiding in het noorden van ons land, bizonder in Groningen," *Gereformeerd Theologisch Tijdschrift*, October 1933, 285.

Koene Vanden Bosch

Another matter that needed his guiding hand—a matter that had been simmering for years—was the matter of Vanden Bosch and the Zeeland congregation. The Zeeland group had originally been part of the Noordeloos congregation, but many members living in Zeeland wanted to form their own congregation and call their own pastor. Vanden Bosch insisted that he was the pastor of all those belonging to the Noordeloos congregation, whether they lived in Noordeloos or Zeeland. At the classis meeting a committee, under the leadership of Vander Werp, was formed. Three days later, October 18, 1864, the matter, after lengthy discussion, was resolved amicably with the Zeeland group being granted permission to call its own pastor.

People soon realized that Vander Werp was a man they could respect and accept as a leader.

Vander Werp's workload grew increasingly. At the January 1865 classis meeting, when the Zeeland church asked for a counselor, he was appointed. He was also appointed clerk for the classis. Considering that in only a few short years the number of churches had gone from four to thirteen, and that all communication was done by letter, the clerk's task was demanding and time consuming.

When Grand Haven sought to organize, Vander Werp was delegated to officiate.[7] In May he organized the congregation of

---

[7]   CRC Classis Minutes, January, 1865, Article 24.

Paterson, New Jersey, and in November, Market Street in Holland. This meant that the Christian Reformed Church now was present in the city of Holland, together with Van Raalte's Pillar Church and the Dutch Presbyterian Church. It is not recorded whether Vander Werp and Van Raalte ever met, but in a town the size of Holland, it would be difficult not to cross paths. Any greeting between the two would have been no more than a perfunctory nod, for as far as Vander Werp was concerned, Van Raalte had commandeered the Holland Classis to join the Reformed Church, and thereby betrayed the people he was supposed to have led. And as far as Van Raalte was concerned, men like Vander Werp lacked a spirit of cooperation and "fanned the fire of distrust and suspicion."[8]

By early 1866, the three pastors, Vander Werp, Vanden Bosch, and Van Leeuwen, were shepherding seven churches (Grand Rapids, Graafschap, Holland, Zeeland, Noordeloos, and Vriesland, Michigan; and Paterson, New Jersey; Polkton had returned to the Reformed Church). Of the three leaders, Vander Werp was clearly the most statesmanlike and the wisest. That is why in 1865 he had been appointed to head a committee to form the church in Paterson, New Jersey, and why the classis also appointed him to go to Pella, Iowa, at the request of some people there eager to organize a church. Furthermore, at the January 1865 meeting, he was also charged with the theological training of Harm Lukas to prepare him for the ministry.[9] At the October classis meeting, John Schepers was added and a pattern formed whereby Vander Werp would take on the apprenticeship of young men—for which he received no remuneration.[10]

In 1866, two years after coming to America, Vander Werp had an opportunity to see the prairies. Early in August he traveled to Pella, Iowa, where he had been invited by about twenty-five families to discuss separation from the First Reformed Church in Pella. After preaching to this group on the Sundays of August 5 and 12, he organized the Christian Reformed church in that city.

Grievances voiced by these Pella families against the Reformed Church included negligence in following the three forms of unity, the

---

[8]   Swierenga, *Family Quarrels*, 87.

[9]   CRC Classis Minutes, January 1865, Article. 17. Harm Lukas does not appear to have completed his training since his name does not appear again in the minutes.

[10]   John Schepers began his studies a year earlier, with Van Leeuwen, but was transferred to Vander Werp at this meeting. Six of his students were admitted into the CRC ministry: John Schepers, Willem Greve, Leonard Rietdijk, Bernard Mollema, Eppe Vander Vries, and Jan Stadt. Others who began their studies with him completed their courses with Professor Boer at the newly established theological school.

use of choirs, singing English hymns, the publication of Sunday school literature jointly with other denominations, admittance of members of other denominations to the Lord's Supper, and bringing corpses into the church for the purpose of holding funeral services.[11] These last two grievances, corpses in church and funerals conducted from the church, had their roots in the Protestant Reformation. Because the Roman Catholic Church insisted that the corpse be brought into the church sanctuary so that a solemn mass for the dead could be celebrated and prayers said for the soul of the departed, Protestants wanted to shun these death rituals and forbade funeral services in the church. The Synod of Dort stated that a funeral was a family affair, and, although not proscribed by Dort, Protestant families customarily invited their pastors to speak words of comfort and admonition at a family gathering in the home of the deceased before burial. These home funeral practices were adhered to in the Netherlands until well into the twentieth century. However, in America, where families were scattered and a church building was a convenient central place to meet, it seemed more practical to conduct funeral services in a church. Nevertheless, Dutch immigrants, who had grown up believing that corpses did not belong in the house of worship, considered the practice yet another sign of laxity.

Even though they had known each other in the Netherlands, Hendrik Scholte, Pella's founder and erstwhile friend of De Cock, did not greet Vander Werp with open arms. In fact, Scholte had developed a deep disdain for the Christian Reformed Church. This is what he wrote about the denomination in 1868:

> We cannot conclude any different than that denomination which deceives itself and others with the title of *ware gereformeerde kerk* [True Reformed Church] is the wickedest district in the contemporary Babylon, with its choking atmosphere destroying the spiritual life and hindering spiritual maturity in grace...a lantern without light and a temple without God.[12]

While it is obvious that Scholte had no use for Vander Werp, Vander Werp for his part would not have made a courtesy call on Scholte either. Scholte was, after all, the man who long ago had dismissed the

11 Jacob Vander Zee, *Hollanders of Iowa* (Iowa City: State Historical Society of Iowa, 1912), 305, 306.
12 Schaap, *Family Album,* 121.

Dortian Church Order—and, more personally, had advised De Cock not to ordain him.

From Pella Vander Werp traveled to Ridott near German Valley, Illinois, and on Wednesday evening, August 22, 1866, he organized a congregation there as well. The July 16, 1866, consistory minutes of Graafschap reveal that the members were not in agreement as to the length of time the pastor should take for this trip, but finally left it up to him. Since Gerritdina was nursing a new baby at this time, it is tempting to visualize Jan Hendrik traveling with his brother. But there are no records to substantiate this.

Back in Michigan, Vander Werp organized a Christian Reformed congregation in Niekerk, September 25, 1866. With the addition of Pella, Ridott, and Niekerk, the denomination numbered twelve

John Schepers, First Minister Trained by Vander Werp

When John Schepers finished his studies with Vander Werp, he became the first minister trained and ordained by the Christian Reformed Church. Born in Hijken, Province of Drenthe, the Netherlands, May 25, 1837, he came to America with his family as a lad of twelve in 1849. The family settled in the vicinity of Drenthe, Michigan, where John experienced all the hardships of pioneer life. He married Jane (Jantje) Rabbers, and together they had one son. By 1864, the fledgling Christian Reformed Church was in dire need of pastors and its classis made an appeal to anyone desiring to be trained for the ministry to apply. At that time John was twenty-seven years old, a farmer, and mourning the loss of his young wife. He applied, was accepted, and began his studies with the Reverend W. Van Leeuwen. When, a year later, Van Leeuwen moved to Paterson, John moved to Graafschap to continue his training with Vander Werp. After four years of study, he was examined and declared a candidate at the September 1868 classis held in Noordeloos, Michigan. He served the churches of First Chicago (now Berwyn), Illinois (1868-1871); Lafayette, Indiana (1871-1876); Ackley, Iowa (1876-1882); and Vogel Center, Michigan (1882-1902). He died in Vogel Center August 13, 1902. His and his second wife, Johanna Van Strien, had seven children: four sons and three daughters.

congregations by the end of 1866.[13] Fortunately, more help was on the way with the coming of William Frieling, another sound and solid pastor from the Netherlands.[14]

At the classis meeting of September 1866, Vander Werp suggested publishing a children's catechism and Sunday school materials to counteract the tracts and Sunday school materials put out by "American" churches.[15] At the same meeting a discussion took place about the viability of a monthly newsletter for the denomination. Vander Werp was asked to look into the cost of having one published for each member of the denomination. At a subsequent meeting he reported a tally of nearly three hundred signatures. However, the vast amount of work generated by the growing number of congregations prohibited a publication—there simply was no time.

All the same, the classis kept coming back to the idea of some sort of newsletter, and two years later Vander Werp was asked to be in charge of it. In 1867 he launched a trial publication, called *De Stem uit het Westen*, or *The Voice from the West*. It only survived for one issue. But the matter of a denominational newspaper was revived when at the January 1868 classis meeting, Cornelius Vorst accepted the responsibility of printing. By February 1868, *De Wachter* had come into being, with Vander Werp as its editor.[16] He received no income from this position but was allowed to keep all the periodicals from other denominations and other news organizations which *De Wachter* received in exchange.

Although he was stretched to the limit of his work capacity, Vander Werp believed that educating the members of the church via their own publication and countering voices from other religiously affiliated papers took precedence over his own comfort. From then

[13] In December 1866 the young denomination considered the following congregations as legal entities of the Christian Reformed Church: Graafschap, Grand Haven, Grand Rapids, Holland (Market Street), Low Prairie (South Holland, Ill.), Niekerk, Noordeloos, Paterson, Pella, Ridott, Vriesland, and Zeeland. These twelve congregations were served by four ordained pastors: Vanden Bosch, VanderWerp, Van Leeuwen, and Frieling.

[14] Like Vander Werp, Frieling had been trained by another pastor. He had served churches that Vander Werp had known, such as Sappemeer, Groningen, and Burum, Friesland. Vander Werp may well have urged Frieling to come and help this fragile denomination.

[15] CRC Classis Minutes, September 1866, Article 18.

[16] Robert Swierenga, *Immigration Records: Dutch in America, 1800*. Family Tree Makers CD. #269. Cornelius Vorst was born in 1825 at Zaandam, the Netherlands; he is listed as *Afgescheiden* and merchant when arriving in Holland, Michigan, in 1855. In 1860 Census of Holland, he is listed as "editor."

on, *De Wachter* became a regular voice for the church. The words on the masthead spelled out its mission clearly: *"In het belang van de Ware Hollandsche Gereformeerde Kerk,"* i.e., "In the interest of the True Dutch Reformed Church." The word *Wachter*, or Watchman, comes from the text printed on the left side of the title page just below the heading, "What I say to you, I say to everyone: 'Watch.'"[17] On the right side of the page on the same level another text reads, "It is written: 'I believed; therefore I have spoken.' With that same spirit of faith we also believe and therefore speak." In the first (and only) edition of *Stem uit het Westen*, publisher Vorst announced that anonymous divisive material would not be accepted; the writer had to take responsibility for his opinions.[18] Half a year later Vorst, apparently annoyed with the number of anonymous items coming in, warned again, "If you wish to see your piece published you must give your name, or at least initials."[19]

The True Brethren strove to defend the truth against all comers using *De Wachter* as their polemic battleground. Van Hinte states, "Strongly opinionated articles appeared especially during its early years. They stormed violently at believers of other religious views, but also members of their own church were taken to task."[20] At one point, even Vander Werp had had enough—in the October 9, 1868, issue he wrote, "I could say much against Rev. De Beij's article in *De Hope* of September 30, but will leave that for his own accountability. I declare at this time that I do not have the desire to constantly argue with people as to who will have the final say, as this serves no purpose and only pleases the devil, because it keeps us from filling the pages of *De Wachter* with more important and worthwhile articles."[21]

With the added responsibilities of editing a biweekly paper, Vander Werp asked the September 1869 classis to release him from his position of clerk. Classis approved the request.

The same classis (September 29 and 30, 1869) also returned to a topic discussed in April 1869 to draft a petition to the state government to reinstate capital punishment. Michigan had abolished capital punishment March 1, 1847—the first state in the Union and English speaking territories to do so.[22] It is not clear why some twenty-two years

---

[17]   Mark 13:37 NIV. In Dutch: "'t geen ik u zegge, dat zegge ik allen: Waakt."
[18]   C. Vorst, "Aan het Publiek," *Stem uit het Westen*, Vol. 1, No. 1.
[19]   *De Wachter*, Vol. 1, #4, March 27, 1868.
[20]   Van Hinte, *Netherlanders*, 449.
[21]   *De Wachter*, Vol. 1, No. 18, October 9, 1968.
[22]   CRC Classis Minutes, April 28, 1869. Art. 26.

after the law had passed in Michigan, the classis wanted a reversal. One reason may have been that the subject was much under discussion in the Netherlands that same year.[23]

The Reverend F. B. Hulst, pastor at the Market Street Christian Reformed Church in Holland, Michigan, had been assigned to draft a document, but he asked to be excused due to his lack of familiarity with the English language.[24] The task was then assigned to Vander Werp, who was to be assisted by his deacon, J. W. Garvelink, a township supervisor.[25] In January 1870 the draft was completed, read by Vander Werp, and approved.[26] However, it appears that it was not sent to the state legislature because at the December 5, 1870, Graafschap consistory meeting, J. Garvelink brought to the floor of the consistory a request to have the classis make a decision to send the petition to Lansing and to hand it to the governor personally. The consistory approved the request, and Classis Michigan, convening in Holland on December 7 and 8, 1870, voted to send the petition to the governor of the state.[27]

The petition raises the question of how proficient Vander Werp became in the English language. Did he read the draft in English? In some of the minutes he recorded in Graafschap there are errors in the spelling of English words. Since most of his congregants spoke Dutch, there was very little incentive for him to learn the language of his new homeland. Any engagement in political activities, however, would have necessitated citizenship and may have been the reason he applied for citizenship while living in Muskegon.[28]

The assembly also tackled the question of fire insurance. This matter had come up as early as 1865, when elders were found to have insured their property against fire damage. They were warned immediately to cancel the insurance and repent of their "sin." To carry insurance was considered a lack of trust in God. Many of the same people who opposed insurance were also against installing lightning

---

[23]   Te Velde, *Anthony Brummelkamp*, 456. Valken, *Kroniek*, 738. The death penalty was abolished in the Netherlands in 1870.

[24]   Hulst (1827-1873) had been in the U.S.A. only since 1868.

[25]   Swierenga, *Immigration Records*. Probably Jan Willem (John William) Garvelink who came to America in 1847 at the age of twelve. In the 1860 Census he is listed as a farmer living in Fillmore Township. He would have been fairly well versed in the English language.

[26]   CRC Classis Minutes, January 19, 20, 1870, Article 15.

[27]   Graafschap CRC Minutes, December 5, 1870, and Classis Michigan Minutes, December 7 and 8, 1870.

[28]   Michigan State Archives, Index to Declaration of Intention 1859-1941, Volume 81.

rods on their barns. By October of 1865, the consensus was not to deny the Lord's Supper to members carrying insurance, but to deny them the office of elder or deacon. In other words, the classis left the decision up to individual church members. But in 1866 there was yet another vehement debate about insurance at classis, and in January 1867 the debate included a discussion whether to insure church buildings. Finally, at the September 1870 meeting, the decision stood to leave it up to the individual believer to decide whether to carry fire insurance. The classis refused to get involved any further in the issue. When the great fire of 1871 destroyed much of Holland, many people unfortunately did not have fire insurance. Vander Werp's position on this issue is not known. (After his death, Gerridina did support the practice. In an 1895 letter to her son John Dirk, she reminds him to pay the insurance on her house, which had come due.[29])

While editor of *De Wachter*, Vander Werp came in contact with another editor, John Y. DeBaun, pastor of the Hackensack True Reformed Dutch Church and editor of the *Banner of Truth*, which he had founded in 1866. Like Vander Werp, DeBaun had not received a formal high school and college education but had been trained by other clergymen. Although born in the United States, he still retained the Dutch language and became an avid reader of *De Wachter*. The correspondence that ensued turned into a life-long friendship. When DeBaun learned that Vander Werp was training young men for the ministry, he sent him a box of Dutch theological books for use by the students. Vander Werp so appreciated this gesture that he wrote about it in *De Wachter*, encouraging other readers to follow DeBaun's example. These books became the nucleus of the Calvin College and Seminary library.[30]

While the books were welcome, Vander Werp's more immediate desire of a seminary for the young denomination encouraged him to raise the subject at the classis meeting of June 1870. One of the arguments he presented was that his own congregational work suffered on account of the time he spent training students.[31] But after some discussion, the classis decided that the church was not able to afford a

29   Vander Werp-Lokker Collection, Calvin College Archives.
30   Willis P. De Boer, "First Editor – My Great-Grandfather," *Banner*, July 1, 1966, 26-27; See also J. A. Westervelt, "A Brief Memoir of Rev. J. Y. DeBaun," *CRC Yearbook*, 1902, 75-80. DeBaun became pastor of the Fourth Christian Reformed Church in Grand Rapids in 1887.
31   CRC General Assembly Minutes, June, 15-16, 1870, Article 32.

seminary and asked Vander Werp to continue the work. Vander Werp was then asked to leave the room. While he was out, a resolution to give him $50 for his work passed unanimously. A year later in June 1872, Vander Werp asked again if there was no one else who could take over the task of preparing young men for the ministry. Again, the answer was "not yet." A year later, the General Assembly of 1873 did vote to give him $75 for all his teaching work to date, and from then on he received $100 annually for his labors.[32]

Congregations Organized by Douwe J. Vander Werp

May 4, 1865	First Paterson, New Jersey
Nov. 8, 1865	Central Ave., Holland, formerly Market St.
Aug. 12, 1866	Pella, Iowa
Aug. 22, 1866	Ridott, German Valley, Illinois
Sept. 15, 1866	Niekerk, Holland, Michigan
Oct. 18, 1866	Oostburg, Wisconsin
July 4, 1867	Cincinnati, Ohio
Oct. 26, 1867	Muskegon, Michigan
Feb. 25, 1868	Collendoorn, now East Saugatuck, Holland, Michigan
April 9, 1872	Cleveland, Ohio, East Side & West Side

---

[32]   CRC General Assembly Minutes, June 1873.

CHAPTER 18

Muskegon

In 1834, when Vander Werp's life had been absorbed in the Secessionist movement in the Netherlands, Lewis Baddeau opened a trading post in Michigan, near a river the French named *Masquignon*, Indian for marshy river. From this small beginning, a community called Muskegon developed into a major sawmill center; it was incorporated as a village in 1861 and as a city in 1869.

By that time many Dutch immigrants, mostly from Vander Werp's home province of Groningen, had found employment in the lumber and sawmill industry. By 1859 their numbers had grown sufficiently to start a church, and the First Reformed Church in Muskegon was organized in June of that year. In 1867 four men—Gerrit Yonker, Egbert Van Baalen, John Waalkes, and Derk Sjerda—met together and voiced their desire to have a Christian Reformed church in Muskegon. Van Baalen was dispatched to the classis meeting held in Noordeloos on October 3, to invite a pastor to Muskegon to organize a Christian Reformed church. The classis delegated the task to Vander Werp, who traveled to Muskegon October 26, 1867, to organize the group, which by this time had grown to nineteen families.[1]

---

[1] Franklin Everett, *Memorials of the Grand River Valley* (Chicago: Chicago Legal News, 1878), 455. Original members were M. Alting, W. Bakker, J. Boersema, J. Boogema, G. Heeres, C. Knijpers, P. Knijpers, J. Langeland, S. Langeland, J. Medema, J. Mulder, J. Pasma, J. Pothof, W. Schuitema, D. Sherda , J. Tempel, O. Timmer, E. N. Van Baalen, and J. Waalkes.

157

One of the founding members, Derk Sjerda, had recently moved from Grand Haven to Muskegon to open a cartage business. He offered his newly built barn on the corner of Spring Street and Muskegon Avenue as a meeting place. The meeting in Sjerda's barn brought back many memories, both for Vander Werp and for Derk. Derk had been a young lad when his father, Kornelis Sjaarda, had taken him along to the clandestine meeting in the barn of the Ellens's farm in Burum, Friesland, where De Cock had preached so powerfully on that June morning back in 1835.[2] Now, so many years and miles later, they were again meeting in a barn, only this time in America, where they were free to worship without fear of fines or governmental persecution.

During the winter months, when it became too cold to hold the worship services in the barn, the congregation met in Yonker's home. As more people arrived and joined, they moved their meeting place to "Peck's Stairs" on Sanford Street, and still later they met in the school house on Terrace Street, which also served as the court house. In 1868 the congregation was able to build its first building on the corner of Apple Avenue and Jay Street. Two years later, young Leonard Rietdyk, Vander Werp's son in law, became the congregation's first pastor.

When Rietdyk moved to Vriesland, Michigan, in 1872, the congregation invited Vander Werp to be its pastor.[3] He accepted. Indeed, for the Vander Werps, moving to Muskegon was a bit like going home. Elders Tempel and Yonker both came from Uithuizen, Vander Werp's hometown. Many of the other members—the Boersemas, Medemas, Klonts, Waalkeses—came from the province of Groningen as well. The Goudbergs and Sjerdas hailed from Burum, his last congregation in the Netherlands.

Perhaps by accepting the call to the smaller Muskegon congregation, Vander Werp intended to scale down his workload. However, his students packed up and moved to Muskegon as well.

Gerritdina wrote about their ministry in Muskegon,

> The small church grew and both pastor and congregation were happy with each other. An addition to the church soon had to be built and two happy years passed. Shortly after this your father became ill and it was found that he had cancer in his mouth. This

---

[2]   In America, Derk's last name was changed from Sjaarda to Sjerda.
[3]   Muskegon CRC Minutes (not dated), Call letter dated June 12, 1872.

was very difficult and painful. We had much anxiety and we tried many means and so-called cures but nothing seemed to help.[4]

Shortly before or after moving to Muskegon, Vander Werp had suffered an accident. On a preaching trip to Vriesland, his horse bolted, throwing him from the carriage. The fall resulted in excessive bleeding from his mouth. He continued with the worship service, but several women in church gave up their handkerchiefs to stanch the flow of blood. It is not known whether this was the onset of the cancer, or whether the wound would not heal because there was a pre-existing cancerous condition. We now know that there is a correlation between smoking, chewing tobacco, and cancer. Vander Werp, like most of his contemporaries, smoked—a habit learned at an early age and not discarded in the new land. Adrian Van Koevering states, "The Dutch pioneers, as a rule, were quite addicted to the use of tobacco. Many pioneers both smoked and chewed tobacco. Peerless Tobacco being the favorite of the masticators was carried in a decorated metal box in the hip pocket."[5]

Before and after church, in consistory rooms, wherever they could, the men smoked. In Graafschap, the horse barn had narrowly escaped burning to the ground several times because of sparks from pipes and cigars. In order to prevent a major disaster, placards were posted on all the barn doors warning church members that entering the barn with lit pipes or cigars was prohibited.[6] According to popular wisdom, the smoke of tobacco pipes warded off mosquitoes, and chewing tobacco alleviated toothaches.

Of all the trials and difficulties Vander Werp endured during his life, this one surely caused the most anguish in body and soul. One of his students, Geert Broene, wrote about this time,

> In the winter of 1874-1875 my tutor became uneasy about a growth in his throat. He and his wife went to Grand Rapids for a medical examination. Three physicians examined him. All three agreed he was suffering from cancer. They even consulted a woman quack in Ridott, Illinois. Two attempts to burn out

---

[4]   Vander Werp-Lokker Collection, Calvin College Archives.
[5]   Adrian Van Koevering, *Legends of the Dutch* (Zeeland, Mich: Zeeland Record Company, 1960), 422.
[6]   Graafschap CRC Minutes, September 14, 1871.

the cancer were so painful that a third treatment was never administered.[7]

At the time, the only relief from pain came from narcotics, since the practice of medicine was just beginning to move away from folk remedies. There were no established medical standards; anyone could open an office—the only limitation was finding sufficient clients.

In fact, a parishioner in Graafschap had tried to alleviate her pain and illness by consulting a somnambulist, or sleep doctor. In the nineteenth century the term somnambulism included hypnotism. A delegate from Graafschap brought the matter to the classis, and inquired how to deal with this particular member. It turned out she was not the only one, but that there were more members of other congregations who did this. The classis considered this an unlawful practice, just like Saul going to the Witch of Endor, and the delegates were advised to report to their churches that those engaging in this practice would be barred from receiving Communion.[8]

With hypnotism not an option, Vander Werp may have tried laudanum, a solution of alcohol and opium, which was the painkiller of choice at the time. The addictive nature of laudanum had not yet become a cause for concern; the fact that toward the end Vander Werp moved in and out of consciousness may well suggest that the drug was administered to him.

By March 1875, Vander Werp had given up the editorship of *De Wachter* for health reasons.

Thereafter *De Wachter* reported regularly on the state of his health:

> May 13, 1875: Rev. D. J. v d Werp's condition is improving.
> May 27, 1875: Rev. D. J. v d Werp is almost completely healed.

With the cancer seemingly in remission, he was able to travel to Chicago to attend the synod held June 2 and days following. Vander Werp opened the gathering with prayer, and in an address to the delegates, expressed his gratitude to God for his healing. A rousing "Amen" arose from the gathered assembly, as all the members rejoiced with him. Another note of gratitude came during the afternoon session when four young men presented themselves desiring to study for the

---

[7]   Geert Broene, *Autobiography of Geert Broene,* translated by Johannes Broene (Grand Rapids: privately printed, n.d.), not paginated.

[8]   CRC Classis Meeting, 21 February, 1866, Article 12.

ministry—one of them being Johannes Vander Werp, Jan Hendrik's son. Since his own two oldest sons had not shown any interest in the ministry, it must have been gratifying to Vander Werp to have a nephew follow in his footsteps. Johannes may have had a few sessions with his uncle during the following months, but he finished his studies with G. E. Boer at the newly formed theological school in Grand Rapids, Michigan.[9]

Later that month, Vander Werp was still well enough to officiate at the wedding of his son, Jan Dirk, to Hiltje Warmink June 27, 1875.

As the summer advanced, however, so did the cancer. *De Wachter* of July 8, 1875, reported:

> According to the latest information, Rev. D. J. v d Werp's illness is not improving. He is gradually getting weaker. Rev. Vander Werp has rejected the proposal to go to a doctor and cauterize the cancer again, as it appears not to have helped and he is afraid he would succumb under the pain. May we carry each other's burdens and pray much for this afflicted family.

Nevertheless, at his physician's advice, he did undergo a second treatment to have the cancer cauterized. The *De Wachter*, August 5, 1875 reported:

> These past days, the disease of Rev. D. J. Vander Werp of Muskegon has taken a very adverse course. Any hope of a speedy and total recovery has not, up until now, manifested itself. The cancer is recurring again and although the physician is using all the appropriate means at his disposal with care and accuracy, these means have not had their desired effect. According to the physician, the problem is that the location of the cancer—under the tongue—hampers the application of the medicines. On Wednesday, July 14, the cancer was cauterized again. Especially since then, Brother Vander Werp is suffering severe pain. We do not have to be reminded that this is a severe ordeal for the Reverend and family. Complete healing now seems more and

[9]   Johannes Vander Werp served the following churches: Overisel, Mich., 1884-1887; South Olive, Mich., 1887-1889; Englewood, Chicago, Ill., 1889-1892; Allendale, Mich., 1893-1895; New Era, Mich., 1895-1898; was ill for a number of years; Falmouth, Mich., 1902-1909; Cincinnati, Ohio, 1909-1911; Luctor, Kan., 1911-1914. At Luctor he had a dispute regarding the prayer in the Form for Baptism, which led to his resignation. See *CRC Acts of Synod,* 1914, 1916.

more doubtful. Nevertheless, the Lord is in control. May he give our brother the grace and patience to bear this awful suffering. May the Lord strengthen him and his wife during this time of testing. And may all the Lord's children add their prayers for those who are being tested. May the Lord grant a favorable outcome, and may this matter result in His Name's honor and grace for the heart and blessing for the congregation.

De Wachter, September 2, 1875: "According to the latest reports, the pain is increasing and he is not sleeping well, so that the Reverend will not be able to attend worship services this Sunday."

De Wachter, September 30, 1875: "Reverend D. J. Vander Werp's condition remains unchanged."

Geert Broene, Vander Werp's student, continued to recount how, as his teacher became increasingly unwell, he would ask Broene to substitute for him at church services, at funerals, and visiting the sick. Broene was asked to do this so often that his own studies began to suffer, and he and another student, Cornelius Bode, went to the manse and discussed the situation with Vander Werp. Vander Werp then advised them to go to Grand Rapids to begin their studies with G. E. Boer, which they did.[10]

The following annual General Assembly dealt with the issue of Vander Werp's retirement and replacement, since there was no longer any doubt that his condition was terminal.

Vander Werp had often used impending death as a wake-up call to those who had not yet come to full faith. He also liked to write in *De Wachter* about the testimony of those who had passed away. For instance, in the first issue of the year 1870, using the text of Jeremiah 18: 16, he wrote in an editorial, "This year you will die. Of course I cannot predict that it will happen to you this year; but this I can say, this year you may die." Vander Werp knew whereof he spoke—during his life, he had experienced at first hand death's intrusions in his life, when it had taken away one loved one after another.

Even so, it must have come as a shock when in November, 1875, he learned that his brother, Jan Hendrik, always in robust health, had passed away after only a day or two of stomach pains. Jan Hendrik—who had gone before him to America—now had gone before him to his eternal home. It is doubtful whether Douwe's condition allowed him to attend his brother's funeral.

---

[10]   Broene, *Autobiography*, not paginated.

On January 16, 1876, he wrote a final farewell message to his congregation. In it he spoke of his pain, "My tongue refuses to let me speak, and my mind can no longer concentrate, and my hands shake too much to write."[11]

It was left to Gerritdina to nurse this man who had been such a tower of strength for all around him. Her sister-in-law, Cornelia, was grieving her own husband's death; her mother was too old and frail to be of any help. The children at home were still too young. She may have had some help from her own Ten Brummelaar siblings, who over the years had one by one immigrated and lived in the West Michigan area.

By February the *Grondwet* reported, "Rev. D. J. VanderWerp is losing ground as the cancer is gaining, and most of the time he is not aware of his surroundings."[12]

It is not recorded how conscious he was at the time when elders E. Langeland and M. De Vries returned from the General Assembly held in Chicago February 2, 1876, with their report. After twelve years of faithful presence at each general meeting, this was only the second one he had missed since his illness. At the last meeting he had requested emeritus status and was awaiting the news. The status was granted. Also granted was an annual emeritation stipend of $300 to be paid in installments every other month. This retirement amount would be raised by scheduling two collections per year.

A fitting tribute to Vander Werp, the man and his work appeared as an addendum to the minutes. No doubt the elders carried a copy of that addendum with them for Douwe to read personally. It read

> Much beloved brother in the Lord Jesus Christ! May the God of all comfort grant you and yours an all-sufficient portion of comfort. Your request for emeritation (at our Classical Assembly in Michigan) we had reluctantly anticipated, since we knew of your suffering and since we received your written request at the above named assembly in December 1875, which grieved us very much. But with all willingness Classis granted (according to Art. 13. of the subsequent decisions of the National Synod of Dordrecht, 1618-19) its approval and since the General Assembly of our church on this continent was approached, this matter was

---

[11] "Mijn tong weigert mij reeds te spreken, mijn hoofd kan niet veel meer bijeen brengen, en mijn handen beven om te schrijven."

[12] *De Grondwet*, March 21, 1876. "D. J. v/d Werp word zwakker en de meesten tijd heeft zijn eerwaarde geen geregelde kennis meer."

presented by our Classis and sincerely supported. Your inability to carry on the ministry due to much suffering from cancer of the mouth causes us much sorrow. But we look back on your labor, in our old fatherland and the years in this land (North America), during which you with your gifts and talents attempted to build up God's Kingdom, and that neither the fruits of your labors, or the strife, have been left behind.

Oh dear Brother, we most gladly give you your emeritation (just as we do) as an honorable discharge of your services. At the same time we promise you and yours an annual stipend of $300, that is, three hundred dollars. And should the Lord restore you to health so that you can work again (which however we do not expect), then you are hereby given complete freedom to resume your work of preaching the Gospel, and you will again be declared eligible for call, and should we hear this, it would fill us with sincere joy. But above all it is our desire and wish that the God, whom you have served, may richly comfort and strengthen you in your difficult suffering. May he grant you and yours a view of his holy sovereign will. And when the time comes for you to exchange the temporal for the eternal, may He grant you an abundant entry into eternal rest. In the name of the General Assembly, held February 2-5, 1876. Rev. G. E. Boer, president, Rev. J. Noordewier, clerk.[13]

The elders also shared other news. The meeting had decided to form a theological school and had chosen Boer as its first full time professor. A Groninger like Vander Werp, Boer had received his training at the Kampen Theology School. He was a logical and fitting choice. Finally Vander Werp's dream of a reputable school for his students and all those desiring to enter the ministry had become a reality. He had run the race, remained faithful, and served the church to his utmost.

The March 2, 1876, issue of *De Wachter* reported that the condition of the Reverend D. J. Vander Werp was "most pitiable. According to one report a large hole has formed in his tongue."

By the end of the month, the March 30 issue reported that his condition was deteriorating, but that he was at peace, though most of the time unconscious. On April 1, he was released from all pain when he entered eternity.

---

[13]   Certificate for the emeritated minister, Rev. D. J. Vander Werp, as evidence of honorable completion of his ministry in the True Dutch Reformed Church in North America.

Tribute from Classis Hackensack

Classis Hackensack, (of the True Reformed Dutch Church) upon learning of Vander Werp's death, issued the following resolution:

> Whereas, the Classis has learned, from Rev. L. Rietdyk, of the sore affliction and death of our brother, D. J. Vander Werp, and realizing the truth of the words of the apostle, that when one member of the body suffers all the members suffer with it, we deeply sympathize with our brethren of the True Reformed Holland Church in the loss of a fellow laborer in the vineyard, who has for so many years usefully, and very acceptably, taught and preached, standing firm for the truth of the gospel to the end, and whom we had learned to honor and love.
>
> Resolved: That we tender our sincere sympathy to the church, and our condolence to the mourning widow and children, hoping they may be supported by a firm trust in a covenant God, who has said, "I will never leave thee nor forsake thee," and who, according to his promises, wills that when his servants' work is done they may be with him to behold his glory for ever. "For them to depart and be with Christ is far better."
>
> Resolved, That this notice be published in the *Banner of Truth* and *De Wachter,* and a copy sent to the widow.[14]

Vander Werp gravesite in Graafschap, Michigan

---

[14]   Minutes Classis Hackensack of TRDC (True Reformed Dutch Church), April 16, 1876, Article VII.

Epilogue

Instead of *Son of Secession*, perhaps this book should be titled *Son of Secessions*, because three times in his life Vander Werp chose to side with a group of seceders. First he joined De Cock in seceding from the Reformed Church in the Netherlands in 1834. Three years later, he seceded from that group, to join the *Kruisgezinden*, and when he immigrated to America in 1864 he joined the Christian Reformed Church, the church that had seceded from the Reformed Church in America in 1857.[1] Did this pattern of reverting back to the older, more orthodox form of church government, preferring strict adherence to rules over a more lenient interpretation, mean Vander Werp had difficulty changing viewpoints? Or was his a true concern for the purity of the church?

In 1856, he along with K. J. Pieters and J. R. Kreulen wrote a 212-page book titled, *Apologie: is de Afscheiding in Nederland, van het Hervormd Kerkgenootschap, zools het thans en sedert 1816 bestaat, uit God of uit de menschen? (Apology: is the Secession from the Reformed Church in the Netherlands, as it [Reformed Church] is currently and has been since 1816, from God or from man?)* From his writing in the *Apologie* we learn that for Vander Werp tolerance toward other viewpoints took second place to the purity of the body and fellowship with Christians not belonging to the *Afgescheiden*.

---

[1] See chapter 8 for an explanation of the *Kruisgezinden*.

B. De Groot, a Dutch historian who studied the book, credits Vander Werp with writing Chapter 4.[2] In this chapter Vander Werp tackled the question of whether it is possible for true believers of the Reformed Church to live in spiritual fellowship with those who in their lives and their teaching deny the confessional statements of the church. His answer is a resounding no. Spiritual fellowship can and should only be with like-minded people who subscribe to the same confessional standards and creeds. All areas of church life, from the preaching of the Word to the sacraments and to the enforcement of discipline are compromised when "true believers" and the less orthodox worship as one body.[3] He cites numerous New Testament texts such as 2 Corinthians 6:14: "Do not be mismatched with unbelievers. For what partnership is there between righteousness and lawlessness? Or what fellowship is there between light and darkness?"

Hendrik Algra, another Dutch historian, noted that the book made quite a stir in Friesland. Vander Werp, he claimed, was without doubt a gifted man. According to Algra, Vander Werp belonged to the *Groningen* (northern) wing, which was suspicious of the *Gelderse* (southern) wing of the denomination and even after the founding of the theological school in Kampen, Vander Werp was not entirely innocent of keeping some of the controversial fires smoldering.[4]

One controversy centered around Anthony Brummelkamp's son-in-law, Jan Van Andel, a theology student in Kampen, where Brummelkamp taught theology. As a trustee, Vander Werp was present at the final examinations of the school in April 1860.[5] After Van Andel had finished his studies he accepted a call to Alkmaar, which belonged in Classis Enkhuizen. This classis, upon examining him, found his theology lacking, thought he had *Remonstrantse* leanings (see

---

2   B. De Groot, "Douwe Johannes van der Werp, 1811-1876: Een Cocksiaan van het eerste uur," *Jaarboek voor de geschiedenis van de Gereformeerde Kerken in Nederland,* D. Th. Kuiper et. al. eds. Jaargang 3 Kampen Kok, n.d. 17 – 41. De Groot credits Pieters with writing the first three chapters, Vander Werp chapter 4, and Kreulen the last two.

3   Vander Werp, D. J. "Of het mogelijk is, dat de ware belijders der Gereformeerde Kerk in kerkgemeenschap kunnen leven met de zoodanigen, die de leer dier kerk, in hare Belijdenisschriften vervat, in leer en leven openlijk verloochenen," in K. J. Pieters, D. J. van der Werp, and J. R. Kreulen, *Apologie: is de Afscheiding in Nederland, van het Hervormd Kerkgenootschap zooals het thans en sedert 1816 bestaat, uit God of uit de menschen?* (Franeker: Telenga, 1856), 95-117.

4   Algra, *Wonder,* 199.

5   Te Velde, *Brummelkamp,* 248. Trustees, with the help of the professors, administered the final candidate examinations each year.

introduction), and would not admit him. Van Andel then accepted a call to Zutphen, where Classis Varsseveld upon examination allowed him to be ordained.

Nevertheless, Van Velzen and Helenius De Cock (son of Hendrik), both professors at the theological school; G. Vos, an elder; and two of the trustees, one of which was Vander Werp, spoke to Van Andel about his leanings. According to De Cock, Van Andel denied man's total depravity, man's inability to do any good, and irresistible grace. As one of the northern wing of the *Afgescheiden*, Vander Werp felt he needed to take measures against these heresies creeping into the *Afgescheiden* church. Because Brummelkamp sided with his son-in-law and could find no fault with him, Vander Werp denounced Brummelkamp's theological leanings in letters to Dirk Postma in South Africa.[6]

Vander Werp carried these controversies with him to the United States, where he complained that the new pastors coming from Holland (meaning those who had studied with Brummelkamp in Kampen) were less than sound in doctrine. "It does not surprise me when I realize how Brummelkamp has overshadowed the entire [*Afgescheiden*] church in the Netherlands with his viewpoint," he wrote to Postma.[7] It was evident, Te Velde notes, that the *Groningse* brothers distrusted Brummelkamp's teaching of dogmatics and his position regarding church order.[8]

Vander Werp also made his position clear in *De Wachter* of February 12, 1869, in which he entered a discussion going on at the time about whether all denominations should unite to form one evangelical denomination and give it a name such as Christian or Bible Church. Using up three columns of the first page, Vander Werp argued against such a union, basing his case on the Heidelberg Catechism, the Canons of Dort, the Belgic Confession, and the Dortian Church Order. "These," he wrote, "are called the forms of unity because they contain the confession of the Reformed Church which every member must embrace and which each minister has to obey; so that no minister

[6] Te Velde, *Brummelkamp*, 284-85. De Beij and Zwemer, *Stemmen*, 153.
[7] Dirk Postma Collection, The Library of the Gereformeerde Kerk, Potchefstroom, Vander Werp to Postma, letter dated January 30, 1867. "Doch het verwonderd mij niet als ik in aanmerking neem hoe dat Brummelkamp met zijne rigting de kerk in Nederland overvleugeld heeft." Algra, *Het Wonder*, 199.
[8] Te Velde, *Brummelkamp*, 246. "Het was duidelijk dat de Groningse broeders zowel dogmatisch als kerkrechtelijk vooral Brummelkamp wantrouwden." De Haas, *Voorgangers*, 1: 132. Vander Werp was not alone in his mistrust of Brummelkamp's theology. His erstwhile instructor, Tamme F. De Haan, also spoke out against Brumelkamp at a trustees' meeting October 12, 1859.

has the freedom to teach otherwise while no member may disseminate teachings that are in conflict therewith or in case they do they must be tried and if they persist they must leave the church or otherwise be cast out."[9]

First and foremost then, Vander Werp's vision of the church from his earliest years to the end was based solidly on the three forms of unity, and the Dortian Church Order. Everything else he considered to be *Remonstrants*, which had no place in the "true church." That this resulted in a denominational *laager* mentality that others viewed as a form of exclusivism he considered inconsequential.

In America, he also found likemindedness with those pastors who had seceded from the Reformed Church in America in 1857, such as Vanden Bosch and Van Leeuwen. In the first sentence of his letter of secession to the classis of Holland, Vanden Bosch wrote, "By this I notify you that I can hold no ecclesiastical communion with you, for the reason that I cannot hold all of you who have joined the Dutch Reformed Church (he means Reformed Church in America) to be the true church of Jesus Christ."[10] Note the phrase, "true church." Klijn, defending the secession of the Grand Rapids congregation from the Reformed Church, wrote, "The Church, The Bride of Christ, is a garden enclosed, a well shut up, and a fountain sealed."[11] In other words, a closed entity, not open to communion with others.

Another aspect of Vander Werp's single-minded vision of the church is worth considering. As De Cock's aide-de-camp he had caught his master's vision of building a "true church." During the first exhilarating years of the *Afscheiding*, many congregations, in spite of persecution, joined this "true church." However, in a matter of years internal discord did more damage than the persecution had done, and by the 1860s many concessions had been made in order to preserve unity and peace. From his correspondence about Brummelkamp, it is evident that Vander Werp began to surmise that the *Afgescheiden* church in the

---

[9] D. J. Vander Werp, *De Wachter*, Vol. 2, No. 1, February 12, 1869, 1. "Deze worden formulieren van eenheid genoemd, omdat daarin begrepen is: de belijdenis van de Gereformeerde Kerk, waarmede ieder lidmaat vereenigd moet zijn en waaraan zich ieder leeraar heeft te houden; zoodat het geen leeraar, vrijstaat anders te leeren, noch geen lidmaat betaamt daarmede strijdige stellingen te verspreiden, of de zoodanigen moeten behandeld worden en daarbij blijvende die kerk verlaten of anders uitgeworpen worden."

[10] *Classis Holland Minutes*, 240.

[11] Ibid., 241. Klijn is quoting Song of Solomon 4:12. He later repented and returned to the RCA.

Netherlands was on the wrong path. Could he perhaps have harbored the hope that in America he could again bring about what had been lost in the Netherlands, just as his colleague, friend, and fellow letter writer, Dirk Postma, had succeeded in doing in South Africa?

Postma and Vander Werp had much in common. Both were from laboring backgrounds—Dirk had been a tinsmith like Vander Werp's father—and both had been trained privately by other clergy. Together they had served as delegates to various synods (at the 1846 synod Postma had served as president, Vander Werp as clerk), and both had been trustees of the theological school in Kampen. Dirk's third wife had passed away in 1857, Vander Werp's in 1858. The 1857 synod had delegated Postma to go on a fact-finding tour and to do missions for the Nederduitse Reformed Church in South Africa and report back. Instead Postma, sympathetic to the needs of a group of dissenters who were against the perceived liberalism of the Reformed Church in South Africa, seceded with them and organized the Gereformeerde Kerk in Suid-Afrika (De GKSA), based on the three forms of unity and the Dortian Church Order. As the only pastor of this newly formed denomination, he trained the first clergy and later founded a theological school. Thus, in South Africa, Postma was able to preserve his vision of the "true church" by passing on his theology to the next generation of church leaders.[12]

Vander Werp and Postma corresponded regularly and Postma's example in South Africa may well have inspired Vander Werp to accomplish the same objective in America—to shape a "true church" by strict adherence to the Heidelberg Catechism, the Canons of Dort, and the Belgic Confession, as well as the Church Order of Dort.[13] Looking at it from Vander Werp's perspective, his dogged perseverance at insisting the Christian Reformed Church abide by these standards makes very much sense.

Douwe Vander Werp's singleness of purpose, his unshakable faith in what he believed, his formidable debating skills, his lucid writing, his organizational skills, his ability to handle his sometimes obstreperous colleagues—all of these were truly godsent for the young Christian Reformed Church at the time of its greatest struggle to survive. His significance to the Christian Reformed Church is undisputed. Without

[12]   DeHaas, *Voorgangers*, 1:211. Just as it dealt with the 1857 secession in the United States, so the *Afgescheiden* Church in the Netherlands, citing lack of information, would not condone or condemn Postma's 1859 secession in South Africa.

[13]   Postma Collection, Vander Werp to Postma, letter dated January 3, 1868.

his leadership, and his vision of what constituted the church—a body of true believers—the young denomination might not have survived. If Hendrik De Cock may be considered the Saint Paul of the Secessionist movement, then surely Vander Werp may be likened to Timothy, his faithful worker in the kingdom.

Chronology
Douwe Vander Werp (1811-1875)

Date:	Event:
May 15, 1765	Jan Hendriks Huizenga and Zwaantje Jans (maternal grandparents) marry in the Reformed Church in Veendam, province of Groningen.
June 22, 1776	Douwe van der Werp from Leeuwarden and Grietje Staats from the city of Groningen (paternal grandparents) marry in the Reformed Church in Groningen.
1785	Catharina Huizenga (Douwe's mother) is born in Uithuizen, province of Groningen.
1789	Johannes Douwes Vander Werp, Douwe's father, is born.
1795	France invades the Low Countries; separation of church and state ensues.
1805	The Batavian Republic is dissolved; the Kingdom of Holland is established.
	Louis Bonaparte, the brother of Napoleon, is installed as king.
1806	New Public Education Law goes into effect.
1809	British troops invade province of Zeeland and hold it until 1810.
1810	The Kingom of Holland is dissolved, and the territory annexed to the French Empire; the provincial

	(or departmental borders) are changed and the provinces renamed; compulsory conscription plan is introduced; all males twenty to twenty-five years of age are registered; the first local population registers are prepared.
June 10, 1810	Johannes Vander Werp and Catharine Jans Huizenga marry in Uithuizen.
Apr. 11, 1811	Douwe Johannes Vander Werp is born in the city of Groningen.
1811	Those without fixed surnames are required to adopt them; this requirement produces the name adoption (*Naamsaangeving*) registers that cover the time period of 1811 to 1813 and 1825 to1826. Civil and church vital records are ordered to be deposited for storage in the local registries. Burials in church buildings are forbidden. Civil registration is introduced in the late fall of 1811; until 1813 and 1814, the recording is often in French.
1812	Napoleon marches to Moscow; only a few of the 15,000 who participated survive; the economic situation becomes so dire that nearly forty percent of the population receives some kind of public assistance.
1813	France withdraws from the Netherlands; C. K. van Hoogendorp sets up a provisional government; Prince William VI of Orange-Nassau becomes King William I and a new constitution is adopted.
1815	Jan Hendrik Vander Werp is born; the national militia is organized, generating militia registers.
1816	New Church Regulations are adopted for the *Gereformeerde Kerk* and renamed *Nederlandse Hervormde Kerk* or Dutch Reformed Church.
1816	"*God zij met ons*," "God with us," phrase added to newly minted guilders.
1818	Hendrik Vander Werp is born.
Feb. 9, 1818	Zwaantje Jans, Douwe's maternal grandmother, dies.
Nov. 12, 1823	Jan Hendriks Huizenga, Douwe's maternal grandfather dies.
Nov. 20, 1824	Wobbenius Rienerwerf Vander Werp is born in Uithuizen.

1825	*Maatschappij van Weldadigheid*, Beneficial Society, rounds up orphans from the entire country and sets them to work in the society's newly founded poor colony in Veenhuizen, Drenthe, resulting in great numbers of deaths of children.
1825	Serious flooding, especially in the northern provinces.
1826	High mortality rates due to fevers and flu; 1,400 deaths above average in Friesland; Woudsend, Friesland, loses half its population; doctors from as far away as Brussels are asked to help.
1828	Continued rains ruin the hay crop, damage the grain and fruit crops, and float away the peat and turf.
May 27, 1829	Willem Johannes Vander Werp is born.
1829	Douwe begins teaching career in Houwerzijl, in province of Groningen.
1829	The Kingdom of the Netherlands conducts its first national census.
June 30, 1829	Gerritdina Ten Brummelaar is born in Kampen, province of Overijssel.
1830	War with Belgium begins; war ends with Belgium's Independence in 1839.
1832	Cholera epidemic; comets; damaging fall storms; King William I initiates a prayer service on Dec. 2; many sermons preached and in print calling the people to repentance, many calling the storms the "rod of God over the Netherlands."
1833	De Cock suspended from his church duties; Douwe dismissed from teaching.
Oct. 1834	*Afscheiding*, or separation of members of the Dutch Reformed Church, takes place in Ulrum, province of Groningen; the separated form their own church.
Nov. 1834	De Cock begins his three-month jail sentence in Groningen.
April 8, 1835	At meeting in Groningen of all *Afgescheiden* congregations, De Cock is appointed their pastor at 700 guilders annually and free housing.
June 21, 1835	First *Afgescheiden* congregation in Friesland is organized in Burum.

1835	Vander Werp is employed as *oefenaar* in Uithuizermeeden, in Groningen; on August 3 preaches his introductory sermon on 1 Pet. 5:10, 11.
Nov. 7, 1835	Vander Werp and Martje Hendriks Van Dam marry in Uithuizen.
Mar. 2-12, 1836	First Synod of the *Afgescheiden Kerk* held in Amsterdam with Hendrik Scholte serving as president.
Aug. 28, 1836	Vander Werp's first son, Johannes Douwes Vander Werp, is born.
1836	Synod of *Afgescheiden* churches make decision not to ordain oefenaars; De Cock serves as clerk; all *Afgescheiden* ministers are present.
Dec. 1836	Martje Harms Van Dam dies.
1836	In November and December Cock travels throughout Friesland to organize churches.
1837	Queen Victoria is crowned in England; much unrest there and on continent.
Oct. 29, 1837	Abraham Kuyper is born in the Reformed parsonage at Maassluis.
1840	William I abdicates and his son William II becomes king.
1841	*Diligence* (stagecoach) service is begun between Leeuwarden and Lemmer.
1841	A call for teacher applicants, third stage, at annual salary of 225 guilders is made.
Aug. 27, 1842	Hendrik Vander Werp and Ludewina Hendriks Jonker marry.
Nov. 1842	De Cock dies and T. F. de Haan carries on with instruction of theological students in Groningen.
29 Nov. 1843	Vander Werp and Albertje Reinders Boersma marry.
1844	Vander Werp is called to serve church in Leeuwarden.
Jan. 9, 1844	Johannes Vander Werp, Douwe's father, dies in Uithuizen. Immigration to United States begins and registers are compiled until 1878.
Mar. 20, 1844	Vander Werp is examined and ordained into the ministry.
1845	Potato crop failure causes near famine, with terrible poverty and looting of bakery stores in the larger cities of Groningen and Friesland; the distribution

	of grain is handled by the government, which also provides employment through work projects.
1847	Reinder Douwes Vander Werp is born in Leeuwarden.
1847	Jan Hendrik, wife and children immigrate to America.
July 9, 1848	Jan Douwes Vander Werp born Leeuwarden.
1848 –1849	Cholera epidemics claims 23,000 lives during 1848 and 1849.
1848	The constitution is revised, allowing freedom of religion.
1849	William III is crowned king.
Aug. 16, 1849	Vander Werp's brother, Hendrik, dies, leaving son Hendrik who later becomes minister in the Christian Reformed Church in America and editor of *De Wachter*.
1850	Population registers commence on a national basis. The population of Friesland is 227,859 of which 205,670 are Protestant; 20,017 Roman Catholic; 1,945 Jews; and 227 have no religious affiliation. Train service between Leeuwarden and Harlingen begins.
June 10, 1850	Catharina Jans Huizenga dies.
Aug. 30, 1850	Catherine Douwes Vander Werp born in Leeuwarden.
Nov. 6, 1850	Grietje Vander Werp (Douwe's sister) marries Lui Bottema.
Mar. 3, 1851	Reinder Douwes Vander Werp dies in Leeuwarden.
April, 1853	The Roman Catholic Church is reorganized, calling for the creation of the Archbishopric of Utrecht with bishoprics of Haarlem, 's-Hertogenbosch, Breda, and Roermond. Large-scale opposition ensues.
7 Nov. 1853	Reinder Vander Werp is born in Ferwerd, Friesland.
20 Nov. 1853	Wobbenius Vander Werp marries Christina De Vries in Groningen.
June 1856	Douwe marries Hendrikje Karsten in Meppel.
June 25, 1858	Hendrikje Karsten dies in Broek-op-Langedijk.
May 27, 1859	Vander Werp marries Gerritdina Johanna Ten Brummelaar in Den Helder.

May 1861	Dirk (D. J.) Vander Werp is born in Burum, Friesland.
July 15, 1864	Wilhelmina Vander Werp is born in Burum, Friesland.
Sept. 25, 1864	Vander Werp family immigrates to America.
May 1866	Johannes (John) Vander Werp is born in Graafschap, Michigan.
1868	Vander Werp becomes editor of *De Wachter*.
May 27, 1868	Douwe (George D.) Vander Werp is born in Graafschap, Michigan.
July 13, 1870	William (Wm. D.) Vander Werp is born in Graafschap, Michigan.
1875	An agricultural crisis occurs due to low prices for grain in America.
Nov. 23, 1875	(Sunday) Jan Hendrik Vander Werp dies suddenly, at age sixty.
Apr. 1, 1876	Douwe passes away.
Dec. 30, 1888	Cornelia, Jan Hendrik's wife, passes away.
June 19, 1911	Gerritdina Brummeler Vander Werp dies in Grand Rapids, Michigan.

Interrogation of Douwe Vander Werp, November 11, 1834, in Smilde

1. Q. What is your name and first name?
   A. Douwe van der Werp.
2. Q. What is your occupation and where do you live?
   A. I have been called to teach here by Hendrik Sickens, Luitsen Dijkstra, Jan Hofman, and Jan Adolfs; before this I was assistant teacher in Houwerzijl, Province of Groningen. I lived in Houwerzijl, but for the past six weeks I have not had a permanent domicile. My parents, Johannes van der Werp and Katerina Huizenga, live in Uithuizen and are tinsmiths by trade.
3. Q. Where and when were you born?
   A. In Groningen, the thirteenth of April, eighteen hundred and eleven.
4. Q. For how long have you been in this municipality?
   A. Fourteen days.
5. Q. What did you do during this time?
   A. The first week I did nothing, and Monday, the tenth of this month, I started with this school.
6. Q. Prior to teaching, did you do home schooling in this municipality?
   A. No, not one lesson.
7. Q. What kind of salary are you drawing here as teacher?
   A. Room and board from the parents of the children who attend, and besides that I was to receive one nickel per week per child.

8. Q. What kind of intentions do you have with regard to your school?
    A. To provide a livelihood for myself, and further to teach the children to read and write.
9. Q. Do you think that you will be able to continue with this school?
    A. No, I want to give it up now.
10. Q. Who has provided the school furniture and who provided the children with the necessary school supplies?
    A. The people who called me here provided the furniture; the children take along their own books, they already had them; I provided the pens and paper.
11. Q. Which teaching rank do you have?
    A. The third rank of the Groningen Provincial Committee.
12. Q. Do you have a written contract from these people who hired you?
    A. No, only an oral agreement; the contract has yet to be made up.

From: F. L. Bos, ed. *Archiefstukken betreffende de Afscheiding van 1834*, 4 vols. (Kampen: Kok, 1934), 110. Translated by author.

APPENDIX 3

Farewell Sermon

Farewell to my dearly beloved congregation of Muskegon

Beloved Congregation:

Several weeks ago you were informed that both the consistory and I had agreed to propose to the honorable classis to release me as your shepherd and teacher and afford me emeritus status, which was then endorsed by the classis and approved. And even though, half a year ago, I was able through favorable circumstances to lead you in a worship service and preach on John 14:2 and 3, we were at that time not fully aware that my condition would deteriorate so quickly. To me, as you may have sensed from my words, it felt that it would be the last time I would preach for you, and that I was saying goodbye to you. The thought had occurred to me to supplement that farewell with a message to be read by one of the elders, and because of the severe pains I suffer night and day, and the increasing weakness of my body, I must now hasten to write something otherwise I will not be able to do it. My tongue refuses to let me speak, and my mind can no longer concentrate and my hands shake too much to write.

Now then, beloved congregation, remember that God's ways with us are for our sanctification. The Lord tests us severely, but also gives many and rich blessings to support and comfort me. I thank all of you who shared so much of my suffering, and who still do. Even though God's ways are different from what we expected and desired, God's will is always for the best, and the Lord has given me the grace to be still and to rest in him, and may he also make you submit to his will in this, that I, your pastor, and you my congregation must part; but that relationship will continue for those who fear him. It would be irresponsible for all those whom I have served to be lost.

Remember then, my beloved, that I have been your pastor for the past three years, and that now while experiencing excruciating pain and facing death, I lay down and enter eternity, trusting in that saving gospel of God in Christ which I proclaimed to you. Seek also for yourselves to walk in the way in which to live is Christ and to die is gain. Not through works, but only by grace and faith in Christ's righteousness can we stand before God. If you are one with me in that precious faith, then we will stay united forever, even though we may be separated for a little while. And isn't that underlying expectation to see God and Christ not wonderful, even more so when in grip of suffering and testing, as I find myself.

May the Lord give you, young and old according to the measure of your faith, what you may have to miss from my serving you, to receive richly through other servants, because he said, "I will not leave you orphans, but I will return to you."

I thank the consistory for the help and support that I received from them. [May] the Lord strengthen them in their difficult task. Brothers! Join me in keeping your eye fastened on him. He will not leave you and me.

I ask the congregation to live in unity, to ease the work of the consistory, and so pray and work together for God's favor to again secure a faithful shepherd and teacher.

Oh dear congregation! Receive my thanks for all the demonstrations of goodness we received from you while we were in your midst. I commit myself and my loved ones to your love and sympathy, because I have not yet finished drinking my cup of suffering; the battle has not yet been fought to the end. Pray much for us, and may the Lord give you and us graciously his sufficient and overflowing comfort for Jesus' sake. Amen

Your loving pastor, who because of his suffering must lay down his ministry to you. Farewell!

D. J. Vander Werp, Muskgeon, January, 16, 1876.

From: *De Wachter*, January 20, 1876, translated by author.

APPENDIX 4

Letter to the Reverend D. Postma in Burgersdorp [South Africa]

Graafschap, January 30, 1867

Honorable Fellow Worker in Christ!

May the blessings of him who resides in the burning bush rest upon you and yours abundantly. Amen.

In spite of distance, our fellowship remains intact. You have been much on our minds since your departure and after learning about your experiences in South Africa. It grieved me that I had not heard anything from you and the brothers in South Africa for a long time. My wife and I talked about you often since my wife brought your children to [the port of] Den Helder for embarkation [on the ship to South Africa to join their father]. And even more so now that we ourselves live in this foreign land of North America where we are experiencing the same struggles you encountered with the Dutch Reformed Church in South Africa. For all the above reasons I was glad that at our last General Assembly I was appointed general secretary to write to you in order to establish mutual correspondence and fellowship with your church, a task I readily and eagerly take upon myself. I am now a little over two years in North America, having been called by a church which by now has battled and opposed for nearly ten years all the churches in North America and especially the Dutch Reformed Church, which most Dutch ministers and their congregations have joined. They not only cooperate in mission and tract [distributing] societies while putting aside and hushing up differences in doctrine, but also exchange pulpits and invite each other's members to the Lord's Supper. Everything is allowed and permitted for ministers, elders, and members, like heresies and membership in Freemasonry, but they never exercise any kind of discipline while all kinds of novelties against God's Word are willfully imported. Years of protests have had no effect, in fact, they refuse to consider protests and they say, don't bother us with them. New fads of the day and everything that smacks of novelty is pushed through highhandedly. Our fathers are considered narrow minded. They speak contemptuously about the best God-fearing authors who want to retain the church as a closed communion. Catechism preaching is neglected. Essential truths are hushed up, and as far as possible even openly opposed, while office bearers refuse to sign the forms. Van Raalte and others are part of this confused Babel and are in fact the prime proponents. If the secession in the Netherlands was needful, the secession here is truly crucial. This is the reason why in the eastern part of N. America a large secession took place already in 1822 of many ministers and congregations who today go by the name of True Dutch Reformed Church or *Ware Hollands Gereformeerde Kerk*. I have spoken with their ministers and members with whom we are truly like-minded, except that they are somewhat labadistic when it comes to baptism and accepting members. As a church we are independent from all those denominations mentioned earlier such as Episcopalian, Methodist, Baptist, Presbyterian, both Old School and New School, German Reformed, Congregational, and Dutch Reformed who all associate with each other and maintain fellowship. We can not join any of them because they lack the marks of the true church. We only practice fellowship with churches which hold on to the Reformed doctrines and church order and which we acknowledge as sister churches, since the rest all show Remonstrant errors and live by their own teachings which they try to force on others, including Christ's physical return. I cannot possibly write you everything, one letter could not contain it all. Our church is planning to send a printed protest to all the consistories against the actions of the last synod of our mother-church in the Netherlands, of which we will send you a copy. In it you will be able to read all the reasons for our secession. Because now they have extended the hand of fellowship to Van Raalte and the Dutch Reformed Church with its heresies that Van Raalte disguised, and by doing so they have condemned our secession. Earlier, when our church asked them on three separate occasions, their answer was that they could not judge the matter and stated that they would acknowledge all churches which held to the Reformed doctrines and church order. And if they could only see it now they would have to recognize that they have cooked their own goose, for now they acknowledge ministers which they deposed in the Netherlands because of heresy, and who were dropped as candidates or students in the Netherlands and who could not become ministers there, people like K. van der Schuur, Stobbelaar, etc., all well-known to you. Though I am not surprised when I consider that Brummelkamp and his followers have taken over the church in the Netherlands. Here I am busy night and day. I have had two students now for more than a year and a third one just joined them. I receive invitations from all over to come and preach and to establish new churches. I receive letters from all over that need to be answered, and I have a large congregation of more than two hundred and fifty members who all live in a radius of about three miles from the church, and then I have to look after the other congregations of our church that do not have a pastor. When I came to N. America our church numbered five congregations and two ministers. Now we have fourteen congregations, of which I myself established six, and we have four ministers now, van Leeuwen, van den Bosch, Frieling, and I. Three men in the Netherlands have received calls such as Duiker, Koopman, and de Beer, the last one actually is from Emden, Ostfriesland.

We would also appreciate hearing from you specifically if there is an opportunity there for Bible distribution among the heathen because we have members here who are quite interested in something like that. When I was about to write you I obtained a letter you had written to a member of one of our congregations in Holland, C. Vorst, and in it I read the history of your church from which I derived comfort because it had so much in common with our church. Your experiences are mine. Some invite me to preach, others scorn and despise me and they do so often in weekly publications. The Lord keeps blessing us; he opens the eyes of many, he converts sinners and nourishes and strengthens God's people, and grants us much peace and his presence to experience.

Convey especially the greetings of my wife to your children and in particular to your eldest daughter. I also especially greet you and all the faithful in the country of South Africa, also on behalf of all the brothers in whose name I wrote to your church. Please be so kind when you receive this letter to forward the enclosed to Rev. Beijer.

Your dear brother in Christ, D. J. van der Werp, d.v.m.

My address is Rev. D. van der Werp, Minister in Graafschap, Allegan County, State of Michigan, North America.

From: Dirk Postma Collection, the Library of the Gereformeerde Kerk, Potchefstroom, South Africa. Translated by author.

The Vander Werp Family

Name:	Born/Mother	Place:	Spouse:	Children:	Occupation	Died:
Johannes	Aug. 28, 1836, Martje Van Dam	Uithuizen, Gron. Netherlands	Single		*dragonder* (light cavalry)	Dec. 27, 1864, the Netherlands
Reinder	May 18, 1846, Albertje Boersma	Leeuwarden, Fr. Netherlands	n/a			March 2, 1851, Leeuwarden, the Netherlands
Jan (John D.)	July 9, 1848, Albertje Boersma	Leeuwarden, Fr. Netherlands	1. Jacoba Van Zanten 2. Anna Warrink	5 children	1. farmer in Fillmore 2. furniture store in Muskegon	Nov. 20, 1919 Muskegon, MI
Catherine	Aug. 3, 1850, A. Boersma	Leeuwarden, Fr. Netherlands	Rev. Leonard Riedyk	8 children	pastor's wife	Mar. 27, 1927, Muskegon, MI
Reinder (Rhine)	Nov. 7, 1853, A. Boersma	Ferwerd, Fr. Netherlands	Catherine Johnson	4 children	store in Fremont clothing store	1907 Fremont, MI
Dirk (D.J.)	May 1861, Gerritdina ten Brummelaar	Burum, Fr. Netherlands	1. Jessie Frieling 2. Johanna Smits	Douwe J. VanderWerp Peter D. VanderWerp Mary A. VanderWerp		Sept. 5, 1937, Grand Rapids, MI

Willemina	July 15, 1864, Gerritdina ten Brummelaar	Burum, Fr. Netherlands	John J. Vermeulen	5 daughters		July 27, 1955, Wykoff, NJ
Johannes (John)	May 25, 1866, Gerritdina ten Brummelaar	Graafschap, MI USA	Agnes Vogel	Helen G. Langeland Barbara W. Gilman Agnes M. VanderWerp	lawyer, judge, state senator	Aug. 11, 1939, Muskegon, MI
Douwe (Geo. D.)	May 27, 1868, Gerritdina ten Brummelaar	Graafschap, MI USA	1. Jennie Bosma 2. Johanna Powells	Josephine G. VanderWerp Jeannette V. Hager Wm. A. VanderWerp	city commissioner, mayor	Nov. 18, 1941, Muskegon, MI
Willem (Wm. D.)	July 13, 1870, Gerritdina ten Brummelaar	Graafschap, MI USA	Nellie Schram	D. W. VanderWerp M. J. VanderWerp Mrs. R. VanderWilt	CRC minister	Feb. 27, 1952, Grand Rapids, MI

Bibliography

I. Archival and Public Sources

Archief de Cock, Municipal Archives at Kampen, the Netherlands.

Ryksargyf, Leeuwarden, Friesland, the Netherlands.

Civil Registries of the Netherlands, Family History Library, Salt Lake City, Utah.

Dirk Postma Collection, the Library of the Gereformeerde Kerk, Potchefstroom, South Africa.

Gemeente Archief, Smilde, the Netherlands.

Michigan State Archives, Index to Declaration of Intention 1859-1941.

Paulus den Bleijker Papers, Calvin College Archives.

Vander Werp, Douwe Johannes, Papers, The Archives, Calvin College.

Vander Werp-Lokker, Gerritdina, Papers, The Archives, Calvin College.

II. Minutes of Churches, Classis, and Synods, and Anniversary Booklets

Burum Gereformeerde Kerk, Minutes, Streekarchivarus, Dokkum, Friesland, the Netherlands.

Calvin College and Theological Seminary 125th Anniversary booklet.

Calvin College Semi-Centennial Volume Theological School and Calvin College 1876-1926 (Grand Rapids: The Semi-Centennial Committee, 1926).

Christian Reformed Church Acts of Synod 1866, 1914, 1916. The Archives, Calvin College.

Christian Reformed Church, Classical and Synodical Minutes, 1857-
    1880. English-language typescript in The Archives, Calvin College.
Christian Reformed Church General Assembly Meeting, The Archives,
    Calvin College.
Classis Hackensack of the TRDC (True Reformed Dutch Church),
    Minutes, The Archives, Calvin College.
 Graafschap Christian Reformed Church, Minutes, The Archives,
    Calvin College.
 Graafschap 100th Anniversary booklet, The Archives, Calvin College.

III. Newspapers and Periodicals

De Grondwet, March 21, 1876.
De Wachter, June 10 and July 8, 1969.
Muskegon Chronicle, August 11, 1939.

IV. Published Works

Aalders, M. J. "Het ambsgewaad ter discussie in de kring der
    afgescheidenen." Kuiper, D. Th. et. al. ed. *Predikant in Nederland
    (1800 tot heden). Jaarboek voor het geschiedenis van het Nederlandse
    Protestantisme na 1800*. Vol 5. Kampen: Kok. n.d.
Algra, A. *De historie gaat door het eigen dorp*. Leeuwarden: Friesch Dagblad,
    1956.
Algra, H. *Het wonder van de negentiende eeuw: Van vrije kerken en kleine
    luyden*. 4th ed. Franeker: Wever, 1976.
Algra, H. ed. *Kroniek van een Friese boer: De aantekeningen (1821-1856) van
    Doeke Wijgers Hellema te Wirdum*. Franeker: Wever, 1978.
Anderhalve Eeuw Gereformeerden in Stad en Land. 12 vols. Kampen: Kok,
    1983-1986.
Bakker, W., O. J. de Jong, W. van 't Spijker, and L. J. Wolthuis, eds. *De
    Afscheiding van 1834 en haar geschiedenis*. Kampen: Kok, 1984.
Beets, Henry. *De Christelijke Gereformeerde Kerk in Noord Amerika, zestig
    jaren van strijd en zegen*. Grand Rapids: Grand Rapids Printing,
    1918.
Beets, Henry. *The Christian Reformed Church in North America*. Grand
    Rapids: Eastern Avenue Book Store, 1923.
Bolt, A. *150 Jaar Gereformeerde Kerk Uithuizen*. Uithuizen: privately
    published, n.d.
Bolt, A. *Geschiedenis van Uithuizen van de middeleeuwen tot en met 31
    december 1978*. Uithuizen: Bakker, 1982.

Booy, E. P. and P. Th. F. M. Boekholt. *Geschiedenis van de school in Nederland: vanaf de middeleeuwen tot aan de huidige tijd.* Assen: Van Gorcum, 1987.

Bos, F. L. *Kruisdominees: Figuren uit de Gereformeerde Kerk onder 't Kruis.* Kampen: Kok, 1953.

Bos, F. L. *Kruisdominees: Verhalen uit Afgescheiden Kringen.* 2nd ed. Kampen: Kok, 1982.

Bos, F. L. ed. *Archiefstukken betreffende de Afscheiding van 1834,* 4 vols. Kampen: Kok, 1934.

Bosch, J. *Figuren en Aspecten uit de Eeuw der Afscheiding.* Goes: Oosterbaan & LeCointre NV, 1952.

Botke, IJ. *Gaat, krijgt een boek of pen in hant en oefent daarin Uw verstant.* Groningen: Universiteits-bibliotheek, 1988.

Boven, John H. and Carol G. Boven. *Boven Dutch Apple Pie.* Wyandotte, Okla.: Gregath, n.d.

Bratt, John H. ed. *Christian Reformed Church Worthies: A Series of Biographies.* Grand Rapids: Eerdmans, 1961.

Brinks, H. J. "Germans in the Christian Reformed Church 1857-1872." *Origins,* 9, No. 2 (1991).

Broene, Geert. *Autobiography of Geert Broene,* trans. Johannes Broene. Grand Rapids: privately published, n.d.

Buisman, J. *Bar en Boos, Zeven eeuwen winterweer in de lage landen.* Baarn: Bosh & Keuning, 1984.

Classis Holland Minutes 1848-1858, Translated by a Joint Committee of the Christian Reformed Church and Reformed Church in America (Grand Rapids: Grand Rapids Printing Company, 1943).

De Beij, B. and A. Zwemer. *Stemmen uit de Hollandsch-Gereformeerde Kerk in de Vereenigde Staten van Amerika.* Groningen: G. J. Reits, 1871.

de Cock, H. *Verdediging van de ware Gereformeerde leer en van de ware Gereformeerden bestreden door twee zoogenaamde Gereformeerde leeraars, of: De schaapskooi van Christus aangetast door twee wolven en verdedigd.* Groningen: Bolt, 1833.

de Cock, H. *Openlijk protest en dichtregelen tegen zeker blauwboekje, getiteld: "Wien moet men gelooven den mensch of God?* Veendam: Mulder, 1834.

de Cock, Helenius. *Hendrik de Cock Eerste Afgescheiden Predikant in Nederland.* Delfzijl: Jan Haan, 1886.

De Boer, P. "First Editor – My Great-Grandfather," *Banner,* July 1, 1966.

Deddens D. and J. Kamphuis, eds. *Afscheiding – Wederkeer: Opstellen over de Afscheiding van 1834.* Haarlem: Vijlbrief, 1984.

de Groot, B. "Douwe Johannes van der Werp, 1811-1876: Een Cocksiaan van het eerste uur, " *Jaarboek voor de geschiedenis van de Gereformeerde Kerken in Nederland,* no. 3, D. Th. Kuiper, ed. Kampen: Kok, n.d.

de Haan, Joh. Gedenk Uw Voorgangers, 5 vol. Haarlem:Vijlbrief, 1984.

de Rover-Wijnstekers, Elly, *De Afscheiding van 1823 te Smilde,* Een eindscriptie van de HBO-Theologie te Windesheim, May 2000, published at: http://members.tripod.lycos.nl/veldeling/smilde.htm

Dosker, Henry E. *Levensschets van Rev. A. C. Van Raalte, Uit oorspronkelijke bronnen bewerkt.* Nijkerk: Callenbach, 1893, p.178.

Everett, Franklin. *Memorials of the Grand River Valley.* Chicago: Chicago Legal News, 1878.

Harinck, G. and Kuiper, D. Th. eds. *Anderhalve eeuw protestantse periodieke pers.* Zoetermeer: Meinema, 1999.

Harms, Richard H. (Ed.) *Historical Directory of the Christian Reformed Church,* Grand Rapids: CRC Publications, 2004.

Heitink, Gerben. *Biografie van de Dominee.* Baarn: Ten Have, 2001.

Hofstede de Groot, P. *Wien zult gij gelooven, den mensch of God?* privately published, 1833.

Homan, Gerlof D. *Nederland in de Napoleontische Tijd 1795-1815.* Haarlem: Fibula Van Dishoeck, 1978.

Homan, S. J. Th. "Cocksianen in Drenthe, Gebeurtenissen rond de Afscheiding in Drenthe, 150 jaar geleden," *Nieuwe Drentse Volksalmanak.* Assen: Van Gorcum, 1984.

Homan, S. J. Th. *Het ontstaan van de Gereformeerde Kerk te Leek.* Leek, Bronsema, 1984.

Huizinga, A. ed., *Encyclopedie van voornamen.* Amsterdam: Strengholt, n.d.

Hulsteijn, J. F. van. *De Gereformeerde Kerk te Middelstum 1835-1935.* Middelstum: Gereformeerde Kerk, 1935.

Mulder, L. H. *Revolte der Fijnen: De Afscheiding van 1834 als sociaal conflict en sociale beweging.* Meppel: Boom. n.d.

Keizer, G. *De Afscheiding van 1834: Haar aanleiding, naar authentieke brieven.* Kampen: Kok, 1934.

Keizer, G. "Documenten bezwarend voor het karakter van Professor Hofstede de Groot," *Gereformeerd Theologish Tijdschrift,* no. 9. 1921.

Klooster, Rienk. *Groninger Godgeleerheid in Friesland 1830-1872.* Leeuwarden: Fryske Akademy, 2001.

Koelman, J. *Het am[b]t en de pligten der ouderlingen en diakenen.* 's Gravenhage: van Golverdinge, 1837. Reprinted: Holland, Mich.: T. Binnekant Holland, n.d.

Kok, J. *Meister Albert en zijn zonen: Uit de geschiedenis der Afscheiding in Drenthe.* Kampen: Kok 1909.

Kromminga, D. H. *The Christian Reformed Tradition, From the Reformation to the Present.* Grand Rapids: Eerdmans, 1943.

Kuiper, R. T. *A Voice from America about America.* Grand Rapids: Eerdmans, 1970.

Kuiper, R. T. *Een Tijdwoord betrekkelijk de kerkelijke toestanden in Noord-Amerika.* Wildervank: Van Halteren, 1882.

Lemmen, Loren. "The Early Church at Polkton, Michigan," *Origins,* 12, No. 2 (1994).

Lucas, Henry S. *Dutch Immigrant Memoirs and Related Writings.* Rev. ed. Grand Rapids: Eerdmans, 1997.

Marang, G. P. *De Zwijndrechtsche Nieuwlichters.* Dordrecht: De Graaf, 1909.

Martz, Helen J. *The Family of Dirk J. Ten Brummelaar, 1804-1864.* Evanston: Privately printed, 1981.

Mathijsen, Marita. *De gemaskerde eeuw.* Amsterdam: Querido, 2002.

Mulder, L. H. *Revolte der Fijnen.* Meppel: Boom, 1973.

Oostendorp, Lubbertus. "Principles or Personalities: How Graafschap became Christian Reformed." *Torch and Trumpet,* April 1957.

Penning, L. *Uit mijn leven.* Zwolle: La Riviere & Voorhoeve, n.d.

Pereboom, Freek, H. Hille, and H. Reenders, eds. *"Van scheurmakers, onruststokers en geheime opruijers..." De afscheiding in Overijssel,* Kampen: IJsselakademie, 1984.

Pieters, Aleida. *A Dutch Settlement in Michigan.* Grand Rapids: The Reformed Press, 1923.

Pieters, H. J., D. J. Vander Werp, and J. H. Kreulen. *Apologie: Is the Afscheiding in Nederland van het Hervormd Kerkgenootschap uit God of uit de menschen?* Franeker: T. Telenga, 1856.

Praamsma, L. *Het dwaze Gods.* Wageningen: Zomer & Keuning, n.d.

Reinsma, J. *Scholen en Schoolmeesters onder Willem I en II.* Den Haag: Voorheen Van Keulen Periodieken, n.d.

Riesen, Wouter van. "Eene Friesche vrijage uit Napoleon's dagen" *Stemmen des Tijds Maandschrift voor Christendom en Cultuur,* W. J. Aalders, et al. eds. Zeist: Ruys' Uitgevers-Mij, 1929.

Romein, T. A. *Naamlijst der Predikanten sedert de Hervorming tot nu toe in de Hervormde Gemeenten van Friesland.* Leeuwarden: A Meijer, 1888.

Schaap, James. *Our Family Album: The Unfinished Story of the Christian Reformed Church.* Grand Rapids: CRC Publications, 1998.

Schrijver, Wim. "Kerk Donkerbroek betaalde tabak voor de kerkeraad" at: www.Leeuwardercourant.nl/Artikel/0,4707,23-7-4921-5579-931434||1227,00.html (January 19, 2003)

Speerstra, Hylke. *De Voorbije Vloot, Verhalen en herinneringen van de laatste echte schippers.* Amsterdam: Contact, 2001.

Staverman, M. *Buitenkerkelijkheid in Friesland.* Assen: Van Gorcum & Co., 1954.

Steringa, P. *Nederlanders op reis in Amerika 1812-1860: Reisverhalen als bron voor negentiende-eeuwse mentaliteit,* Utrechtse Historische Cahiers, 20 vols. Utrecht: Universiteit Utrecht, 1999.

Swierenga, Robert P. *Dutch Chicago: A History of the Hollanders in the Windy City.* Grand Rapids: Eerdmans, 2002.

Swierenga, Robert P. *Family Tree Maker's Family Archives, Immigration Records: Dutch in America, 1800s.* CD #269. Broderbund, 2000.

Swierenga, Robert P. and Elton J. Bruins, *Family Quarrels in the Dutch Reformed Churches in the Nineteenth Century,* The Pillar Church Sesquincentennial Lectures, A. C. Van Raalte Institute. Grand Rapids: Eerdmans, 1999.

ten Zythoff, Gerrit J. *Sources of Secession, The Netherlands Hervormde Kerk on the Eve of the Dutch Immigration to the Midwest.* Grand Rapids: Eerdmans, 1987.

Te Velde, Melis. *Anthony Brummelkamp (1811-1888).* Barneveld, De Vuurbaak, 1988.

Tollenaar, F. *Een eeuw kerkelijk leven van de Gereformeerde Kerk te Den Helder.* Kampen:Kok, 1940.

Valken, Maarten. ed. *Kroniek van Nederland.* Amsterdam: Elsevier Boeken, 1988.

Vanderberge, P. N. ed. *Historical Directory of the Reformed Church in America 1638-1965.* New Brunswick: Commission on History, Reformed Church in America. n.d.

van der Does, J. C. *De Afscheiding in haar wording en beginperiode,* 2nd ed. Delft: Naamlooze Vennootschap W.D. Meinema, 1934.

van der Does, J. C. *Kruisgezinden en Separatisten.* Franeker: Wever, n.d.

Vander Werp, D. J. *Lofdicht van een door God geduldig en lijdzaam gemaakten lijder and Geestelijke Wapenkreten en Belijdenis mijns geloofs bij het verdrukken en vervolgen van H. de Cock.* Veendam, Mulder, 1835.

Vander Werp, D. J. ed. *Synodale besluiten des Christelijke Afgescheidene Gereformeerde Kerk in Nederland van 1836-1837: Bijeenverzameld en van een algemene register voorzien.* Kampen: Van Velzen Jr., 1859.

Vander Werp, Henry. *An Outline of the History of the Christian Reformed Church of America*. Holland, Mich.: Holkeboer, 1898.

Vander Werp, Marvin J. "Rev. Douwe Johannes Vander Werp, Eerste Hoofredacteur," *De Wachter*, Feb. 6, 1968.

Vander Zee, Jacob. *Hollanders of Iowa*. Iowa City: State Historical Society of Iowa, 1912.

van Dijk, D. *Hoe het was, en hoe het geworden is*. Goes: Oosterbaan & Le Contre, 1960.

Van Eyck, Wm. O. *Landmarks of the Reformed Fathers*. Grand Rapids: The Reformed Press, 1922.

van Gelderen, J. and F. Rozemond, eds. *Gegevens betreffende de Theologische Universiteit Kampen* 1854-1995. Kampen: Kok, 1994.

van Koetsveld, C. E.. *Schetsen uit de Pastorie te Mastland, Ernst en Luim uit het leven van den Nederlandschen dorpsleeraar*. 7th ed. Schoonhoven: Van Nooten, 1874.

Van Koevering, Adrian. *Legends of the Dutch*. Zeeland, Mich.: Zeeland Record Company, 1960.

van Rijswijk, C. *De Poorten Sions bemind boven alle woningen Jacobs*. Zwijndrecht, Van den Berg, 1983.

Versteeg, Dingeman. *De Pelgrim Vaders van het Westen*, Grand Rapids: Loomis & Co. n.d.

Weerden, J. S. van. *Spanningen en konflikten: Verkenningen rondom de Afscheiding van 1834*. Groningen: Sasland, 1967.

Wesseling, J. *Afscheiding van 1834 in Friesland*. 3 vols. Groningen: De Vuurbaak, 1980-1983.

Wesseling, J. *De Afscheiding van 1834 in Groningerland*, 3 vols. Groningen, De Vuurbaak, 1972-1978.

Wesseling, J. *Afscheiding en Doleantie in de Stad Groningen*. Groningen: Niemeijer, 1961.

Wesseling, J. *Afscheiding van 1834 in Overijssel*. Vol. 1. Groningen: De Vuurbaak, 1984.

Westervelt, J. A. A brief Memoir of Rev. J. Y. DeBaun, *CRC Yearbook*, 1902.

Westervelt, J. A. "Rev. D. J. Van Der Werp," *Banner of Truth*, 39/10, 1904.

Weyde, H. v. d. and H. W. van Egmond. *1840 – 1990 Anderhalve Eeuw Gereformeerde Kerk den Helder: Afscheiding - Doleantie - Vrijmaking*. Den Helder: Gereformeerde Kerk Den Helder, 1990.

Wildeboer, D. R. "Gevangenisstraf in 1852 voor beenderendelvers uit Hallum, Ferwerd, Marrum, Blija en Holwerd," *De Sneuper*, Dokkum: n.p., March, 1999.

Wormser, J.A. *Een Schat in Aarden Vaten, Eerste Serie III "Werken Zoolang het Dag is" Het leven van Hendrik De Cock*, Nijverdal: Bosch, 1915.

Zaal, Wim. *God's onkruid, Nederlandse sekten en messiassen*. Masterdam: Meulenhoff, 1972.

Zumthor, Paul. *Daily Life in Rembrandt's Holland*, trans. S. W. Taylor. Stanford: Stanford University Press, 1994.

Index

Kremer, Klaas, 49
Kreulen, Jan. R., 88, 89, 141, 167
Kropswolde, Province of
    Groningen, 57
Kruid, J., 110n
Kruisgezinden, 59-61, 64, 65, 79,
    91, 92, 99, 105, 109, 113, 117,
    145, 167
Kuipenga, Klaas Pieters, 14
Kuiper, Roelof, 119
Kuyper, Abraham, 103, 123

Labadie, Jean de, 139, 139n
Labadism, 138-140
Lafayette, Ind., 150
Lamberts, Jan, 71n
Langeland, E., 163
Langeland, J., 157n
Langeland, S., 157n
Lankheet, H., 110n
laudanum, 160
Lauwersmeer, 86n
Lauwerszee, 86
Lay preacher, xiii, 25, 40, 41, 43,
    54-56, 59, 74, 79, 99, 132, 140
Ledeboer, L.C.G., 89
Lederboergezinden, 89
Leens, Province of Groningen, 14
Leeuwarden, Province of
    Friesland, xi, 2, 69, 73-77, 79,
    80, 86, 87, 93, 95, 102
Leiden (University of), xix, xx
Lemmer, Province of Friesland, 95
Lijnbaansgracht, Amsterdam, 55
Lioessens, Province of Friesland,
    85-87
Low Prairie (South Holland, Ill.),
    151n
Luctor, Kans., 161n
Ludema, Arjen Kornelis, 86n

Lukas, Harm, 128, 148

Mangel, Jan, 71n
Market Street CRC, 138, 148, 153
Marriage proposal, 93
Marriages, 53, 82
Marriages, ecclesiastical, 71-73
Masquignon, Mich., 157
Mastenbroek, Province of
    Overijssel, 60
Maurik, Province of Gelderland, 143
Measles, 15
Medema, J., 157n
Medemas, 158
Meerburg, George Frans Gezelle, 54
Meijer-Brouwer, Laurentius, 5n,
    8, 17, 19, 21, 22-24, 27, 29, 31,
    33
Mennonites, 7, 103
Meppel, Province of Drenthe, 90
Methodist, 184
Mevrouw, 99
Middelburg, Province of Zeeland,
    139n
Middelstum, Province of
    Groningen, 23, 48, 106, 142
Military, 37, 50, 78, 94, 124
Military draft, 10, 14
Militia, 24
Milwaukee, Wis., 79, 109, 123
Molenaar, Rev., 21n
Mollema, Berend/Bernard, 129, 130
Mulder T.E., 31, 32
Mulder, J., 157n
Muskegon, Mich., xiv, 109, 130,
    153, 155, 157-159, 161, 181
Muskegon Ave., 158

Nederduitse Reformed Church,
    171